Signed,
Your Student

Signed,
Your Student

EDITED BY HOLLY HOLBERT

FOREWORD BY BRUCE A. HOLBERT

New York

© 2010 by Holly Holbert

Published by Kaplan Publishing, a division of Kaplan, Inc.
1 Liberty Plaza, 24th Floor
New York, NY 10006

Printed in the United States of America

Library of Congress Cataloging-in-Publication Data has been applied for.

10 9 8 7 6 5 4 3 2 1

ISBN-13: **978-1-60714-121-1**

Kaplan Publishing books are available at special quantity discounts to use for sales promotions, employee premiums, or educational purposes. For more information or to purchase books, please call the Simon & Schuster special sales department at 866-506-1949.

DEDICATION

This book is dedicated to our parents, Vince and Margaret Moore, Bonnie Hogue, Pat and Barb Holbert, and our children, Natalie, Luke, and Jackson Holbert.

CONTENTS

Signed, Your Student

Contents

PART 2: Middle School and High School

Contents

Contents

PART 3: College

FOREWORD

This book was born in a fashion akin to my first child. The labor pains arrived early in the morning, and I was the last to know.

One December night about two years ago, Holly woke me in the middle of the night. She couldn't sleep. Three nights earlier, a 17-year-old boy at my high school had killed his parents and then come to school as usual the next morning. His mother was a math teacher at a high school where I had worked two years before. She didn't arrive at school that morning, so the police were called to the house to make a welfare check. They found two mutilated bodies inside a tractor's bucket.

> **❝She announced she had decided to write a book for the teachers, 'the ones like you who no one hears about.'❞**

Outside my classroom window, three squad cars surrounded a mid-80s compact in the student parking lot. The number of police officers struck me as unusual. The kids were less surprised. Their speculations ranged from drugs to a stolen ATM machine. None of us yet knew that the police had arrested a boy in the classroom next to my own for double homicide 20 minutes before.

The teachers were called to an emergency staff meeting after the last bell and given the details of the murders. The police and especially the administrators and counselors had handled the situation with a grace and compassion that was remarkable but, because they are remarkable people, not surprising. A counselor who had some connection with the boy called him from class and walked him to the counseling center, where he was interviewed, in part to keep him from the media that had began to gather in the parking lot. His girlfriend was immediately taken by another counselor to make her statement. Neither counselor left the room until each student had indicated he or she was ready to answer police officers' questions.

The student's friends were quietly plucked from different rooms in the building and informed by counselors of the situation. They were given time to call parents and offered support either through the school's resources or professional people within the community. No one else knew of the incident until the kids who were close to the boy had been informed and until the boy had been escorted downtown to be booked.

Later, some of the staff complained about not being notified, but passing the information to us before the police had finished their preliminary work and before the kids with emotional ties to the situation were prepared could have presented a plethora of problems for police investigating the scene and interviewing relevant students; moreover, it would have placed our interest in the situation above those of a number of students whose emotional stake was much higher and who were much more fragile. Thinking back on the incident, my bosses had had a pretty good day in the face of pretty awful circumstances.

The next few days at school were difficult, as you might guess. Teachers hovered, checking on kids who were having a difficult time and collecting funds for the only other child in the family, a 20-year-old girl, who not only had to cope with the loss of both parents but also the fact that her brother had.

When Holly woke me, I remember checking the clock to see if I had slept through the alarm. It was some time after 2:00 A.M., and sleep was at a premium.

She announced she had decided to write a book for the teachers, "the ones like you who no one hears about."

"What?" I asked.

"I was thinking about how you stand out in the hallway between classes to be sure you talk to everybody when they pass by or come into your room. You make jokes with them and check or tease their girlfriends or boyfriends. Kids you don't even have in class stop to talk with you. Most teachers are like that. Sometimes you make people feel better and you don't even know them. I think I want to see if I can find stories of those teachers."

I'm sure I was not terribly encouraging. I may have yawned and thought, *This too shall pass.*

When I next woke, though, Holly was already at the computer, and since then I'm not sure she has spent a stretch of more than 24 hours away from it. She started with a query filled with regard for me and with such honest and sincere language that even if the project had not progressed further, that letter would have been a gift as generous as any I've been given. It seemed to me, though, that that letter's moving qualities spelled out the project's doom. No one would respond to a query that didn't include who would possess the international rights and where each contributor's name might appear on the jacket.

I was wrong.

Stories began arriving a week later. Janet Reno called and I didn't take it because the caller ID read simply "RENO" and I thought she was selling timeshares. The kids raced to the mailbox because no one knew when John Glenn or Beau Bridges or Jim Belushi might drop us a line. Those who could not contribute often wrote or called to encourage the project. This was the most compelling unintended consequence of the book project. People wanted to honor their teachers, yes, but they were just as anxious to respond to Holly's genuine desire to do something of significance for me. What she felt for the work I have cared about and committed to for over 20 years; work that she saw as too often unappreciated, moved the people she solicited in a manner that hundreds of thousands of words directed at the nebulous ideas of teachers in general, or the even more cloudy abstraction of education, could not.

It should not have surprised me. Almost every story in this book is rooted in the context of successful people recalling teachers who were willing to purchase, with time and effort, stock in their lives before they themselves knew they were worthy of the marketplace. As a result, these students purchased larger stakes in their own lives and, for the most part, made good on the investment.

That is the genius of the best teachers. One may teach the most demanding class in the school; another may have little concern for grades at all. But if they are like the teachers in this book, their students understand: these teachers' demands are efforts to demonstrate to the students talents and character they are not yet aware they possess.

Like my daughter's birth, my wife bore the labor of this book and I coaxed a little at the end. However that does not preclude me from having hopes for both.

For teachers, I hope they will recognize themselves in these stories. I can see almost everyone I work with in one or another.

For students and parents, I hope the same, that they will also see their teachers in these pages, because they are there. In my career, I have had the good fortune to teach great kids, almost every one of them. Many are generous enough to write or stop at my classroom as their lives progress and express their thanks. That they take the time to do so doubles the value of any paycheck. For those kids, perhaps, I am the exception, the one who spoke to them for the weeks or months when hearing my voice could move them forward in their lives. Though it would gratify my ego to be the person to whom each responded in such a manner, I know I am not. I take much solace in that knowledge, however, as I consistently witness students in other classrooms captained by other teachers, some polar opposites of myself in our notions of how to run a classroom finding themselves in the same manner they do in my own. I have encountered no one in this profession who has failed to affect at least a student or two in significant ways; most teachers do so every day, just as the teachers in the contents of this book have.

I hope, finally, that if people who have little or no connection to schools stumble upon these stories, these pages will provide enough light to balance the dark aspersions that the media and politics often cast on my profession. I hope, too, that these readers will be reminded of the paradox education researchers consistently report: while respondents claim that educators in this country perform unsatisfactorily, they just as characteristically rate their children's teachers as above average or excellent.

—Bruce A. Holbert

Bruce Holbert earned an M.F.A. in Creative Writing from the Writers' Workshop at the University of Iowa, where he held a Teaching-Writing Fellowship. His work has appeared in *The Antioch Review*, *The Iowa Review*, *Other Voices*, *Crab Creek Review*, *The Inlander*, *Hotel Amerika*, *The Spokesman Review*, *The Tampa Tribune*, and *The West Wind Review*. He has worked for 24 years as a high school teacher in Jerome, Idaho; St. John, Washington; and at Rogers High Schools and is currently teaching at Mt. Spokane High School in Spokane, Washington. He has been married 24 years and has three children.

INTRODUCTION

My husband, Bruce, has been a high school English teacher for almost 25 years. In that time he has received countless letters from students and parents thanking him for the effect he has had on their lives and the lives of their children. But, even with all this gratitude, he still feels almost ashamed when anyone asks what he does for a living.

Every day in the paper, Bruce can read about low test scores, about teachers who are incompetent or take advantage of their students. Letters to the editor typically assail everyone in the profession for too much homework or not enough, for too much discipline or not enough. Recently, our local paper trumpeted the arrest of a sex offender, the headline reading "Local Teacher Arrested for Pedophilia." Only near the end of the article does the reader discover that the offense occurred in the last three months and the offender's teaching career ended 20 years ago.

> **The first year of teaching is legendary for its difficulty. Bruce always says that in his first year of teaching, he learned everything he didn't want to ever do again.**

Signed, Your Student

What we don't hear much about are those many teachers like Bruce who quietly go about affecting thousands of children's lives for the good. Instead of holding teachers in the highest regard and vigorously recruiting the best people for the job, as some countries do, we pay them lower wages than the average college graduate and think of them as hired hands. Teachers like Bruce, it's sad to say, have at times more positive influence on our children's lives than even their own parents do.

Bruce's first teaching job was in Jerome, Idaho. Jerome is a small town of around 7,000 in southern Idaho. His base salary was $8,500 a year, barely enough for rent, food, utilities, and to begin paying off some of his student loans. The high school he taught in was so overcrowded that he had 40 students in his first classroom—and only 30 desks. The first year of teaching is legendary for its difficulty. Bruce always says that in his first year of teaching, he learned everything he didn't want to ever do again.

On his first day, when Bruce was handing out books, a student looked at him mischievously and said, "You've never done this before have you?" He coached three sports and came home exhausted. Even then, though, he seemed to have a knack for thinking of ways to engage kids. He instituted aerobic tardies, requiring calisthenics for anyone arriving late; he created a weekly lottery for students with perfect attendance, the prize being a can of Silly String that they could spray on their peers between classes.

The following year he took a job closer to home, back in eastern Washington. St. John was, and still is, a tiny farming town of 500, nestled in the hills of the Palouse. The English teacher preceding him was 70 years old before the community politely convinced her to step down. I'm sure she would have liked to retire earlier, but the Washington State Teacher's Retirement Fund had gone bankrupt a few years earlier,

Introduction

leaving her with a scant pension. Boys fixed her car, built her tables in the shop, or mowed her yard for grades. The girls apparently were graded on behavior.

Bruce values his subject matter about as much as the rest of us value our money. With a willing group of seniors, who asked only to "learn something this year," he prepared 20 of the 25 for college futures; eventually 18 of them earned B.A. or B.S. degrees, eight earned master's degrees, and one a Ph.D. Consistently, his students returned to say that Bruce's class had taught them how to learn.

I can't remember how many times during that first year in St. John I came home to find him so exhausted he could hardly get off the couch. He wasn't sure if he was being too hard or too easy on them. He didn't know if he was teaching them the things they needed to learn or if they were even "getting it." He still worries about those things throughout every school year. I suppose all great teachers have these worries.

I was at the school one day early in his first year when one of Bruce's students came up to him and said she couldn't read some of the comments he had written on her paper and didn't know why she had only gotten a C.

He said, "Well, maybe you're right. Can I read it again and then talk to you about it tomorrow?"

One of the many things that has always made Bruce stand out among his peers is his lack of ego in such matters. He will always barter a higher grade to a student if it means that that student will feel motivated to continue to meet his high standards and will feel part of what he calls his "community." Whether it is in teaching or in any other part of his life, Bruce is willing to listen and think about the other side. If teachers are always on the defensive and trying to explain their view instead of listening, the students will do the same.

Bruce and I were married his second year in St. John. We lived in a small trailer within walking distance of the school. I remember the two of us sitting in the living room on the night before homecoming and hearing voices outside. The next moment there were 25 kids making a serpentine through our front door and out the back door. Kids called or came over to our house two or three nights a week for one thing or another. He understood them and they recognized that. This is not to say that Bruce was the only person in the school with such traits. He always says and truly believes that most of his motivation is to hold up his end as well as the peers he continues to admire have done.

Bruce has always practiced his craft of writing as well as teaching it. In 1987, he applied to the University of Iowa Writers' Workshop. It's the toughest writing school in the country to get into. At least 700 people apply each year and 25 of those are lucky enough to be admitted into the workshop. When he was accepted, the St. John school board allowed him a nonpaid two-year sabbatical so his teaching job would be there if he wanted it when he graduated. Life at the workshop was everything he had hoped for. He got a chance to live his art and to talk about writing with people who were doing the same. We met friends who have become family to us; all of them encouraged Bruce to go east to New York or to at least stay at the university where he would likely find a teaching job, as he had held the highest fellowship the program offers. But Bruce decided to return to St. John, mostly because he had promised his freshman class he would be back, and also because, though he loved Iowa, he had encountered there the selfishness necessary to practice the arts and he found that isolation lacked a quality of spirituality, which he got from teaching.

Each year the senior class in St. John chooses a person whom they admire to speak at their graduation. Bruce was asked by four different classes to be their speaker in a span of twelve years; when you consider that no person can be asked twice in a row, he was asked more than half the time he was eligible. One of those times was the first year of his sabbatical in Iowa. He had written a letter to the class telling them how proud he was of them and reminded them of some funny stories he recalled. For the first time in St. John High School history, the graduation speech was in the form of a letter written by their chosen speaker (Bruce) and read by the class president.

Fast-forward 19 years: Bruce has published almost a dozen short stories and is completing a novel. He teaches now in a much larger school in Spokane, 50 miles north of St. John. We have three great kids: Natalie is 18; Luke, 17; and Jackson, 15. Bruce still writes when he gets the chance, on weekends and during the summer, if one of the kids doesn't have some event going on. His students, current and former, still call and e-mail regularly. He has paid rent on an apartment for a girl left homeless for four months, helped those wanted by the police turn themselves in with dignity, taken in many, some for a few days, some for months at a time. He's brought food for his pregnant girls and visited his boys in jails and hospitals. He's written hundreds of letters of recommendation for colleges, jobs, and, sadly, to judges whom he must try to convince to coordinate jail sentences with finishing school.

We have been talking for years about writing a nonfiction book together. I would do the research and he would do the writing. When I proposed the book you're now holding in your hands, Bruce was flattered, I think, but had little hope the project would sprout wings and fly. He suggested I contact some local notable people around the Spokane area; maybe one or two of them might give me a story. I began by e-mailing a few local authors. A local juvenile author called me within a half hour of receiving my e-mail. He said he thought it was a great idea and asked how I was going to promote it. I told him my ideas; he thought I was thinking too small. He suggested that I contact people across the country and see what the response was. I could always narrow my scope later if I had a hard time getting stories nationally.

I began sending e-mails and a few letters via the post office the following February. Within a week, Maya Angelou's assistant called. Within three weeks, I had stories from Dionne Warwick, Jerry Spinelli, and Beau Bridges. The response has continued to be amazing. I have received over 75 stories from people in various walks of life. It has been so fun to open up my e-mail and letters every day, not knowing what I will find. I grabbed the mail one day before picking up my three children from school. I shuffled through the mail while waiting for them in front of the school and found a letter and story from former astronaut and senator John Glenn. When my kids got in the car I showed them the letter—it was like Christmas morning for them.

As the stories filtered in, the book's themes began to take shape. The stories were personal and heartfelt. Some people wrote about teachers who had helped guide them through their early-childhood years. Others wrote about their personal struggles and the teacher who had helped them through it. A few wrote about the tough teachers who made a difference, but most wrote about a teacher who changed the course of their lives and are a big reason that they are the accomplished adults that they are today.

Introduction

I want to thank everyone who gave me interviews, snail mailed me, e-mailed me, or allowed me to use their previously published stories. I hope that others, teachers and nonteachers alike, will read these stories and think about those teachers who made a difference in their own lives.

I can say that this project has already given Bruce the personal rewards I hoped it would. He is humbled and warmed by the number of responses and the level of emotion within them. I hope that by presenting the stories in this book, other committed and hardworking teachers (the lion's share of them, Bruce always says), will find solace and feel some of the gratitude of others for their hard work.

I also wanted to thank the teachers who made a difference in my life, but even more importantly, all the teachers, coaches, and school staff who have made a difference in my own children's lives. Thank you to Jeff Baerwald, Jim Bannister, Molly Beil, Jana Berg, Millie Brezinski, Bob Cameron, Carolyn Craven, Tim Cruger, Alana Cummings, Chad Charbeneau, Denise Dalbey, Maria DiBartolo, Ed Drouin, Patty Dudley, Brian Dunn, Maureen Fanion, Sue Grantham, LaShea Hayes, Jim Herling, Kurt Kimberling, Tria Kostelecky, Joe Lefler, Tim McBride, Camille Miller, Chuck Moffatt, Karl Mote, Dave Noble, Dan Nord, Steve Olson, Morris Owen, Peck Dan, George Pettigrew, Jeff Pietz, Robyn Ross, Jeana Simpson, Alecia Sing, Alex Spanos, Angela Spencer, Linda St. Clair, Mark St. Clair, Matt Sullivan, Rob Tapper, Gene Villa, Laura Watson, Kathey Weiss, Joyce Winters, Lori Yonago, and the list could go on and on and on.

Signed, Your Student

Dear Teacher:

Please teach my son.
He will have to learn, I know,
that all men are not just, all men are not true.
But teach him also that for every scoundrel there is a hero;
that for every selfish politician, there is a dedicated leader . . .
Teach him for every enemy there is a friend,
Steer him away from envy, if you can,
teach him the secret of quiet laughter.

Let him learn early that the bullies are the easiest to lick . . .
Teach him, if you can, the wonder of books . . .
But also give him quiet time
to ponder the eternal mystery of birds in the sky,
bees in the sun, and the flowers on a green hillside.

In the school teach him it is far more honorable to fail than to cheat . . .
Teach him to have faith in his own ideas,
even if everyone tells him they are wrong . . .
Teach him to be gentle with gentle people,
and tough with the tough.

Try to give my son the strength not to follow the crowd
when everyone is getting on the bandwagon . . .

Introduction

Teach him to listen to all men . . .
but teach him also to filter all he hears on a screen of truth,
and take only the good that comes through.

Teach him if you can, how to laugh when he is sad . . .
Teach him there is no shame in tears,
Teach him to scoff at cynics and to beware of too much sweetness . . .
Teach him to sell his brawn and brain to the highest bidders
but never to put a price tag on his heart and soul.

Teach him to close his ears to a howling mob
and to stand and fight if he thinks he's right.
Treat him gently, but do not cuddle him,
because only the test of fire makes fine steel.

Let him have the courage to be impatient,
let him have the patience to be brave.
Teach him always to have sublime faith in himself,
because then he will have sublime faith in mankind.
This is a big order, but see what you can do . . .
He is such a fine fellow, my son!

Sincerely,
Abraham Lincoln

Part One
Grade School

ANDREW GROSS

Author, *The Blue Zone*

I Was Your First-Grade Teacher

My fondest memory of a teacher's most meaningful effect on me doesn't go back very far.

As a boy, I went to a small private school outside of New York City. Then (the early 1960s) it was all about tiny classes, woeful athletics, and crew-cut, predominantly Jewish kids whose most flagrant acts of defiance included removing their neckties on school grounds.

> **" 'Do you remember me, Andy Gross?' she asked. "**

First grade—what can I recall except learning the rudiments of arithmetic and penmanship from a kindly Englishwoman named Rosemary Gumpel, who taught us manners and civility and treated us goofy, giggling miscreants in an unnaturally adult way. Truth is, not a single, well-defined scene from that time filters through—other than hiding rock-hard mashed potatoes from the cafeteria in my blazer pocket one day and facing the consequences by being held back from recess. Years later, my penmanship has eroded into an illegible scratch, but I do manage to shift unwanted food to the side of my plate. Amid the memory haze, somehow I know that that June I was jettisoned off to the second grade feeling a bit more individualistic and mature.

Fast-forward 50 years. I was doing a luncheon talk at a local French restaurant, with maybe 30 people in the room. After I finished, an elegant, slightly familiar, white-haired woman stepped up to me.

"Do you remember me, Andy Gross?" she asked.

I looked in her kindly eyes and apologetically shook my head.

She smiled and told me, "I was your first-grade teacher."

Something inside me started to fall apart, like the columns of an ancient temple collapsing at the whim of the gods. I don't know what it was—seeing the long passage of time on Miss Gumpel's face or realizing it was probably showing on my face too. She told me how the years had passed for her, recalling that we were her first teaching assignment, then ticked off incredibly vivid memories of me as a bratty six-year-old: how I was "cute" and "feisty" (*me?*) with impeccable penmanship and how I loved to eat, "though I was so thin." (I decided not to remind her about the mashed potatoes story.) I was always "challenging," she said, "and dare I say it, one of my favorites."

I was stunned that she could pick me out after 50 years. That she could pick up a book in a store, look at the author photo, and recall his traits as a child. I realized that this is what teachers have as their equity: not just names and flickering faces and grades, passed along from year to year, but children, people, recognized and remembered after a lifetime; kids who would leave behind their giggly shells and amount to something: marry, have families, careers, children of their own; and how this long, linear journey started somewhere. She boasted a bit, unaware of the 20 years I'd spent pursuing other dreams: "I always knew you'd become a writer."

I suddenly looked at her and in that instant, realized how much a part of this one woman I had become. It made me hold back tears.

So now my first-grade teacher and I keep in touch. Occasionally I hear updates from some of her other students, classmates of mine who I lost touch with a lifetime ago. And my own memories have come back, of who I was: a gangly stick who became a man, who had a career, raised a family, learned to write books—seen through the prism of a teacher I had long forgotten, who saw promise in a young boy, 50 years before.

Thank you, Rosemary Gumpel.

Andrew Gross is the author of international best sellers *The Blue Zone* and *The Dark Tide*, and coauthor of five No. 1 best-selling novels with James Patterson, including *Judge & Jury, Lifeguard,* and *The Jester.* Gross lives in Westchester County, New York, with his wife, Lynn. They have three children.

MELORA **HARDIN**

Actress, *The Office*

An Arena for Me to Shine

My third-grade teacher was Mrs. Story at Toluca Lake Elementary, a sweet public school in the San Fernando Valley in Los Angeles. At the end of every year Mrs. Story had her children recite their favorite poem in front of the class. Being a professional actress from the time I was six years old, I was very excited about this and prepared long and hard. I wanted to win the prize, any book. I wanted to learn to draw animals. My favorite poem was "The Raggedy Man": "O the Raggedy Man! He works fer Pa; / An' he's the goodest man ever you saw!" I wore my overalls, my mom braided my hair in two braids, and I recited the whole poem with a Southern accent and in the character of a Southerner to go along with it. It was so exciting to be up in front of my fellow classmates doing something I knew I was good at. It was fun and playful and it made me really connect to that poem in a special way. I remember everything about that day and I still remember that poem. I won and I got my book of choice, *How to Draw Animals*, which I still have somewhere. Mrs. Story made an

> **Mrs. Story's creative way of helping us to connect with the words and the meaning of the words will stay with me forever.**

arena for me to shine. I don't think I was the only kid who enjoyed it. It was ingenious to have children memorizing poetry at eight, and it gave me my first taste of what would grow into a real passion for poetry. Mrs. Story seemed quiet to my eight-year-old self. She seemed old and old-fashioned. I wonder now how old she really was. But she had a twinkle in her eye when it came to English, writing, and literature. We could all feel her passion and it was transferred to us kids. I was not an early reader and I believe it was in Mrs. Story's class where I really began to enjoy reading for the story and the essence of the piece and finally got beyond the words and the exercise of reading. Mrs. Story's creative way of helping us to connect with the words and the meaning of the words will stay with me forever. I see that day in my mind's eye as a shining example of how a teacher can positively imprint the mind of a child with joy, curiosity, and excitement. This curiosity and hunger for details and textures has bled over into all that I have read and all that I read now. Teachers have the opportunity to shape and sculpt each generation to be more interested, more imaginative, more specific, and to ask more questions. These are qualities not only for a healthy adult mind but also for a healthy culture and a healthy society. Teachers are heroes!

Melora Hardin is a professional dancer, singer, and actress. She currently appears on *The Office* as former corporate manager Jan Levinson. She also appears in *Hannah Montana: The Movie*.

MARY ANN ESPOSITO

Host and creator, *Ciao Italia*, PBS

Ye Ol' Schoolteacher

My favorite teacher was also my gym teacher, Miss Schibler. I recall her making me stay in for recess to practice cursive writing on the blackboard. It seems I could not get the loopiness of the letter *p* right, so I would trace over and over the model she had on the blackboard. In gym class, she made me practice gymnastics on the horse, which I hated. She knew I was not athletic but she put me on the basketball team anyway! She always believed in me and when I started my own television show 18 years ago, she sent me a knife block with a brass plate below that was engraved, "to my television star from ye ol' schoolteacher, Miss Schibler."

Mary Ann Esposito is the host and creator of PBS's *Ciao Italia* (www.ciaoitalia.com), America's longest-running cooking series now in its 20th year of production. She has authored a dozen cookbooks, including her latest, *Ciao Italia Slow and Easy.*

CECIL **MURPHEY**

Coauthor, *90 Minutes in Heaven: A True Story of Death and Life*

I Didn't Know Her First Name

I never knew Mrs. Leamer's first name, but I remember her well. She became our substitute teacher my first day in third grade. She had light freckles, sandy-colored hair, and thick glasses. When she spoke to me, even at age nine, I felt she directed her attention totally to me.

I can't remember anything Mrs. Leamer taught me; however, I can never forget the lessons I learned. I was a shy, skinny boy whose clothes never fit properly. What few new clothes I had, Mom had bought at a secondhand store or gotten as hand-me-downs from neighbors. Mrs. Leamer didn't seem to pay attention to my clothes; she did pay a lot of attention to me.

> **❝I can't remember anything Mrs. Leamer taught me; however, I can never forget the lessons I learned. ❞**

One Friday she asked me to stay after school. As soon as the other students had gone, she handed me a book. "I took this from the big library for you." Both of us knew that no students checked out books from the big library until fourth grade.

11

"It's written on a fifth-grade level," she said, "but I think you can read it. At least, I'd like you to try."

I stared at the book and read the title: *Father's Big Improvements.*

I thanked her (at least I hope I did) and raced from the room. I didn't even wait until I got home to start the book. As I walked the 11 blocks to our house, I read the first two chapters. I had trouble with a few words, but she was right: I could read the book. Monday morning, I handed it back to her. "It was good. It was about the father who lived on an old farm and put in electricity and learned to operate a gasoline-powered plow."

She patted my arm. "I knew you could read it."

The following Friday after the final bell rang and all my classmates rushed into the hallway, Mrs. Leamer handed me a book. This time she only smiled and walked away. It was Booth Tarkington's *Penrod.*

I don't know how many weeks this went on, but just before Christmas vacation, she handed me another book, a children's version of the Grimms' *Fairy Tales.* "You might want to read this during your vacation."

I smiled gratefully and clasped the book in my hands.

When school started in January, we had a different teacher. I laid the book on her desk when she wasn't looking. I never saw Mrs. Leamer again. I'm sure I missed her, but life moved on quickly for us in third grade.

Long after I became an adult, I thought of Mrs. Leamer. I couldn't remember anything we studied, but I vividly remembered what she did for me. The books, although important, weren't the most important. She made school a haven for me, or as I sometimes think of it today, a safe place.

Without her ever saying such words, Mrs. Leamer made me feel accepted and valued. Obviously, she didn't see only that shy, skinny kid but instead focused on my potential—not just who I was, but who I could be. Home was a house of beatings and drunkenness, a place of yellings and unhappiness. My father drank often and sometimes became violent. That fall a serious, nonalcohol-related illness kept him out of work for months. Yet when I walked into Mrs. Leamer's classroom, I could push that part of my life behind me. For those hours, I escaped from loneliness, poverty, and isolation. I was safe and someone cared about me. Beginning with those days in third grade and continuing all the way through high school, once I walked inside the school building, I tuned out my miserable home life.

Years later, I tried to locate that special teacher; however, the school system no longer kept records dating back that far. Even though she had entered and left my life within a three-month period, Mrs. Leamer had given me hope.

In a way, that's how life operates, isn't it? Through the years, God has sent people into my life—individuals like Mrs. Leamer—to nurture and encourage me. Those special individuals enabled me to inch toward feeling accepted and worthwhile.

I never knew Mrs. Leamer's first name, but I know God does. I felt as if God used several special people to prepare me for wholeness and acceptance. One of those individuals who helped was a woman whose first name I never learned.

Cecil Murphey, also known as The Man Behind the Words, is the author or coauthor of more than 100 books, including the *New York Times* best seller *90 Minutes in Heaven* and *Gifted Hands: The Ben Carson Story.* His books have brought hope, encouragement, and inspiration to countless people around the world. For more information, visit www.themanbehindthewords.com.

DAISY **MARTINEZ**

Chef and host of *Daisy Cooks!*, PBS

The Time I Needed

From grade school through high school, then college, and even culinary school, I have always been blessed to have teachers who are passionate about what they do. It is probably the reason I remember them today: they experienced such joy from what they did.

> **❝I was the only non-English-speaking student, and my poor teacher, Mrs. Sharlon, certainly had her work cut out for her.❞**

Since I never attended kindergarten, and didn't speak English, first grade was a trying experience. I was the only non-English-speaking student, and my poor teacher, Mrs. Sharlon, certainly had her work cut out for her. I remember her standing by my desk, showing me how to fold my paper into four columns, and teaching me what it meant to "vote."

We had a piano in the classroom, and Mrs. Sharlon would teach us songs (which I learned phonetically at first), and then we would skip to the music, single file, around the classroom.

She took the extra time that I needed, teaching me to read, to enunciate, to learn English; most importantly, she taught me a love of reading that I value to this day. There was never a "stupid" question. It was okay to "color outside the lines," and by the end of first grade, I had the highest reading level in the class. I still remember the hug of pride she gave me when my dad and I went in for our Parent/Teacher Conference.

I left P.S. 42 in Staten Island, New York, after the fourth grade, and at that time I wasn't mature enough to let Mrs. Sharlon know the great impact that her love for teaching had on me, but to this day, I remember her kindness, her patience, and the enthusiasm that she mustered each and every day, in front of 24 six-year-olds, one of whom couldn't speak a word of English.

Daisy Martinez is an actress, model, chef, television personality, and author. She hosts the PBS television series *Daisy Cooks!* Her new show, *Viva Daisy!*, launched on the Food Network in 2009.

PATRICK **TAYLOR**

Author, Irish Country Books series

Tell Us a Story

Teaching is an undervalued profession and yet almost everyone owes a great deal to at least one, and often many, of their teachers. In my case the debt is to two teachers whom I remember vividly.

I have had a very satisfying life, first as a research physician in Canada, and in the last ten years as a novelist whose books all have Irish themes. I doubt if I would have followed either path had it not been for the gentle guidance of those very special people.

Maud Tipping taught history at my elementary school and Colin Wilcockson was a high school English teacher.

Because of them I developed a love of learning (a love started by one, which I nearly let slip away, but for the other),

❝ Maud Tipping, Miss Tipping to us children, was a diminutive, gray-haired, unmarried woman who in her middle thirties seemed ancient to a nine-year-old boy. ❞

a deep respect for the English language (encouraged by both), and a lifelong interest (instilled by one) in the mythology and history of Ireland, my native country.

Maud Tipping, Miss Tipping to us children, was a diminutive, gray-haired, unmarried woman who in her middle thirties seemed ancient to a nine-year-old boy. She was charged with instructing us in history; as we lived in Northern Ireland, that part of the island that was and is still an integral part of the United Kingdom, "history" was British history.

Miss Tipping discharged her responsibilities by faithfully drilling us in such matters as the dates of every British monarch from William's conquest in 1066 to the coronation of King George the Sixth in May 1937. She taught us about the battles the Duke of Marlborough won. She did her job well. His victories, if you are interested, were Blenheim (1704), Ramillies (1706), Oudenarde (1708), and Malplaquet (1709). The usefulness of this information is lost on me, but nearly 60 years later I still remember, because Miss Tipping was meticulous in teaching the curriculum as decreed by the Ministry of Education.

But Maud Tipping gave me something of much greater value. She showed me that learning could be interesting; finding out new things, exciting. And what is research? Nothing more than finding out about new things.

Ten minutes before the end of each class she would lower her voice and say, "Now what shall we do, children?" and we would reply, "Tell us a story, Miss."

Maud Tipping brought those stories to life. She would have made a consummate actress if she had chosen the stage. For those ten minutes there would be not a sound but her gentle voice reading to us from a book called *The Knights of the Red Branch,* telling of the adventures of the great Irish hero Cú Chulainn (pronounced Koo-coolin), and of his and his warriors' struggles with the armies of Queen Maeve of Connacht.

Maeve was jealous of her husband Ailell's great bull, Finnbheannach. She determined to steal Donn, the great brown bull of Ulster, and in this she eventually succeeded. When she took Donn back to Connacht he fought and killed King Ailell's animal then made his way back home to Ulster, where he eventually died.

In that one epic were heroes, villains, gods, goddesses, love, hatred, battles, peace, loyalty, betrayal, life, and death—great themes all told lyrically, stories to rival the *Odyssey* or the *Iliad*. And she made one little boy want to learn more, to find out new things about Ireland.

I was nine and she had hooked me for life on Irish mythology, the art of storytelling, and the use of the language to tell those stories. She set me on a lifelong path of discovery.

It was she who brought books from her own library for me to read, she who would stay after class and discuss with me what I had read, help me to understand the finer points of the plots; and show me how the plot is the driving force of a good tale. She taught me by example that learning was fun, not drudgery. And she did it on her own time, without receiving a penny for her troubles.

For all good teachers, who are by far the vast majority, teaching brings its own rewards, more precious than money. Through her efforts I subsequently discovered that *The Knights* . . . was a reworking of that great epic the *Táin Bó Cúailnge* (*The Cattle Raid of Cooley*), Ireland's oldest recorded saga.

She later introduced me to the myth of *The Children of Lir*, where the children are turned by a wicked stepmother into swans and forced to live as swans for 900 years. More love, jealousy, enchantment, not just of the children but of this reader.

From there it was but a short step to finding the poetry of William Butler Yeats, a man heavily influenced by the old Celtic tradition. I have often wondered whether he had *The Children of Lir* in mind when he wrote "The Wild Swans at Coole"; in that poem he says of the birds, "their hearts have not grown old."

I've not had that question answered, but I've been a devotee of Yeats ever since Maud Tipping lent me his collected works. His love affair with matters Celtic, into which he drew John Millington Synge, Lady Gregory, and Connie Countess Markiewicz (one of the leaders of the 1916 Easter Rebellion), soon had enlisted another volunteer. Me.

Every time I write a scene that invokes Irish mythology or history I silently bless Miss Maud Tipping, who lit my interest in it all and for four years kept those fires burning brightly.

But when I turned 13 I didn't bless her for making me a scholar, and the blaze she had ignited almost turned to ashes; indeed I believe it would have—but for one man.

Colin Wilcockson, English master extraordinary.

Boys' boarding schools, like the one I was sent to in Belfast in 1954, were wonderful places for the gregarious, the athletically inclined, the joiners, the average students. Their ethos was taken straight from Thomas Hughes's *Tom Brown's School Days*, Rudyard Kipling's *Stalky & Co.*, and G. A. Henty's tales of derring-do on India's Northwest

Frontier. Stiff upper lip. Good sport. Never tell tales to the masters. Play up, play up, and play the game.

But the game included tormenting, in the argot of the time, "swots": boys who liked to study, the timid, and the athletically disinterested.

By the end of the first year, having failed to distinguish myself as either a rugby player or cricketer, but having a tendency to earn high marks, I had defined myself as the perfect target. And in a closed society there was nowhere to run.

I had no chance to improve athletically: you are either talented or not talented. That route to social approval was closed. If appearing clever led to punishment from other boys, it didn't take a budding genius to work out how he might remove that source of irritation. I let my marks slide. I thought no one would notice; the boys certainly didn't.

But Mr. Wilcockson, my English teacher, did.

After one class he told me to go to his study. In the days when canings were handed out regularly, and for trivial offenses, such a summons was greeted by small boys with all the enthusiasm of a convicted felon when invited to visit the electric chair.

As I walked to his study, I tried to remember what I knew about the man.

He was quiet, small, unassuming. He had fair hair that he wore parted to the right and hanging in a fringe on the left side of his forehead. He was always clean shaven. His eyes were blue and his voice was soft. I never heard it raised in anger. He wore tweed sports jackets with leather elbow patches. There was always a book sticking out of a pocket. I distinctly remember seeing the title of one: *The Hobbit*. His shoes were always highly polished.

I have no idea what he did outside the classroom, other than reading. He may have smoked. Most men did in those days. He may have liked a drink, but I doubt if it would have been more than half a pint. He must have had hobbies, interests. Someone told me he wanted to be a novelist. Like all men he would have had his dreams, his aspirations, his fears, his worries. I don't remember if he was married.

I do remember I was terrified on that particular day. I didn't recognize that it would be a turning point in my life. As I stood outside his door summoning the courage to knock, I did remember how much I enjoyed his classes.

In those days every child in Northern Ireland had to read certain "set" books and assigned plays of William Shakespeare in preparation for a series of nationally set examinations, the results of which predicated whether you might or might not attend university.

Mr. Wilcockson could make *The Woodlanders*, a turgid work by Thomas Hardy, seem fun, and the archaic English of *A Midsummer Night's Dream* a game of code to be deciphered with intense satisfaction the prize for the successful decoders. When it came to teaching grammar and syntax the man could make the language sing and dance jigs. I loved learning from him.

I could guess why he wanted to see me. A recent assignment; I'd botched it deliberately.

I knocked.

He opened the door. "Come in, Taylor." His voice was expressionless. He wore his academic black gown. "Sit there." He indicated a wooden chair.

I sat.

"Would you like a cup of tea? A biscuit?" He indicated a tea service, but I was too scared. I merely shook my head.

"Suit yourself." He poured tea for himself and sat behind his desk.

"Do you know why I sent for you?"

I kept my gaze firmly on the floor.

He handed me sheets of paper. "That's your character study of Giles Winterbourne."

I took the sheets.

"I've read it. I'm not going to mark it. It's rubbish."

I flinched and wondered what was coming next.

"Why is it rubbish, Taylor? You love reading. Understanding characters is easy for you. Why is your work rubbish?"

I swallowed.

He stood and seemed to tower over me so I pulled away, but he fooled me. He came round the desk and squatted in front of me, eyes level with mine. His voice softened. "I'll tell you why."

I looked straight into his eyes. There was a softness in their blue depths.

"You're terrified of doing well . . ."

I nodded.

"Because if you do the bigger boys will pick on you, won't they?"

I nodded and felt the hot tears start.

He stood. "I'm not going to ask you which ones. I went to school. I understand the code. It's like the code of silence, *omertà*, practiced by the Sicilian Mafia. *Omertà*." He walked to a bookshelf and returned with a book. "Read this. You'll enjoy it."

"Thank you, sir." I read the title. *Murder, Inc.,* by Turkus and Feder.

"You should be in it. You've just murdered a character study."

"I'm sorry, sir."

"Sorry, Taylor," he said quietly, "isn't good enough. I want to suggest something to you."

"Yes, sir?"

"Either I give you the mark you deserve, you'll fail the course, and I'll not bother with you again . . . You can go on getting failing marks . . ."

I swallowed. I'd already set my heart on going to medical school, but failure in the national examinations would not allow me to attend university.

"Or you'll go and redo the thing and give it your best effort."

"But . . ."

"And if you're worried about being bullied just remember *I* can be the biggest bully in this school if I think some twerp is affecting someone else's work. And I will be."

He had understood and was willing to take steps to protect me. I could have kissed him. "Yes, sir." I managed a smile. "I'll . . . I'll have another go."

"Good," he said. "Now have some tea."

I accepted.

"And I want you to do something else for me."

"Sir?"

"You have a talent with the words. Work on it, keep working on it . . . and I'll help you."

I did and he did. He could have turned his back on me. There can't be much satisfaction in trying to teach children who staunchly refuse to learn. He didn't turn away. He rescued me from myself at a time when I was ready to give up.

If it hadn't been for Colin Wilcockson I wouldn't have been a novelist and thus wouldn't have been invited to write this piece, where I've been able to describe two teachers who in their own ways were the two greatest influences in my life. To you both, Maud Tipping and Colin Wilcockson, "Thank you very much" and it doesn't come close to expressing the admiration and the gratitude I feel and the debt I can never repay.

Patrick Taylor was born in 1941 and brought up in Northern Ireland. He attended Bangor Grammar School, Campbell College, and the Queen's University of Belfast. After qualifying as a gynecologist in 1969 he pursued a career in academic medicine in the field of human infertility, retiring in 2000 as Professor Emeritus, University of British Columbia, after ten years as head of the department of Obstetrics and Gynaecology at Saint Paul's Hospital, Vancouver. He is now a full-time writer and author of seven works of fiction, including the *New York Times* best seller *An Irish Country Doctor.* He can be contacted at www.patricktaylor.org.

SHERRI **SHEPHERD**

Actor, comedian, and cohost of *The View*

Love for Reading

I remember my fourth-grade teacher, Mrs. Losheska (I'm sure I've butchered the spelling of her name!). I lived in the inner city, so all the little girls looked forward to being in Mrs. Losheska's class, 'cause she was the pretty blond white woman who'd let us comb through her "silky" hair. I'm sure that's why I wear longhaired wigs to this day!

At 4 P.M., Mrs. Losheska would have us all relax at our desks while she read to us. She was a master at voices and would take us to a world seldom explored. I

> **At 4 P.M., Mrs. Losheska would have us all relax at our desks while she read to us.**

remember looking at the clock in anticipation of 4:00, so that I could hear all the different characters in Mrs. Losheska's books. My love of reading was instilled in me by Mrs. Losheska.

To this day, I love to escape in the afternoons with a good book. I love to read to my son. I too use different voices, the way Mrs. Losheska did, and I hope that I too can instill that same joy of reading in my son.

Sherri Shepherd is a stand-up comedian, actress, and cohost on the ABC daytime talk show *The View*. She has a recurring role on the NBC television show *30 Rock*. She was also the voice of lioness Florrie in the film *Madagascar: Escape 2 Africa*.

JANET EVANS

Olympic Gold Medalist in swimming

Mrs. Lane's Olympics

My favorite teacher was Mrs. Lane. I had the pleasure of having Mrs. Lane as my teacher in both the fifth and sixth grades. Both of my older brothers had had Mrs. Lane as their teacher as well. They would come home from school with great stories of what they'd learned in her class and what a great teacher she was, so needless to say I was thrilled to finally be a part of her classroom once I was old enough.

❝Although she didn't know a thing about the sport of swimming, she took me seriously when I told her in fifth grade that I was going to be an Olympic swimmer. ❞

What made her a great teacher was her interaction with the students. She made every one of us feel important in our own way. She took an active interest in our lives and made a point of asking us about things we did outside of school, such as our music lessons or athletic pursuits. She could often be found at our junior high and high school swim meets, football games, and soccer games, cheering on her former students.

Her teaching style made class fun. Everything was hands-on and interesting. Every day in class brought something new and fun, and she even made our boring math homework and tests seem not so drab. Not surprisingly, the thing I remember most about her was her smile—it never seemed to go away.

Most importantly, Mrs. Lane taught me—through example and encouragement—that I could do and be anything I wanted to in life. Although she didn't know a thing about the sport of swimming, she took me seriously when I told her in fifth grade that I was going to be an Olympic swimmer. From that day on, she encouraged me to practice and do my best, even if it meant that I had to leave early from one of her many field trips to make it to my afternoon swim workout.

Mrs. Lane celebrated with my family and friends when I returned home from my first Olympic Games with three gold medals. Her positive attitude and encouragement helped me win those medals when I was still in high school—not too long after I graduated from her sixth-grade class!

I give a lot of credit to Mrs. Lane and will be thrilled if my own daughter is fortunate enough to have a teacher just like her one day.

Janet Evans won three gold medals for swimming during the 1988 Seoul Olympics. She added to her medal count during the 1992 Barcelona Olympics, winning gold in the 800 meter and silver in the 400 meter. Evans participated in the 1996 Olympics but cites running with the Olympic torch as the highlight of that competition.

KERI **TOMBAZIAN**

Voice-over actress

My Wish to Find Her

Evelyn Tabor. Does anyone know of her whereabouts? Back in 1985 when I first wrapped my brain around the World Wide Web, one of the first things I did was try to find her. Mrs. Tabor was my third-grade teacher at Chandler Elementary School in Sherman Oaks, California, 1965. The mark she made on me is best evidenced in my abiding wish to find her.

> **Once, when she caught me in a grandiose lie told to impress my classmates (about cooking a Thanksgiving turkey, of all things), Mrs. Tabor found a way to both make me come clean and save face.**

What are the odds that she, probably now around 70 years old, would remember me: a little girl with nothing particularly special about her, save a deep struggle to be still, to fit in, and to not be sad? I was not one of those kids who jumped right into the public arena with ease. I fretted and worried and resisted the natural ebb and flow of social development. I talked too much, too loudly, and worried so much about fitting in that I learned to sublimate myself and take on the features of my surroundings. Nice trick for a chameleon; hell for a kid. But Mrs. Tabor would have none of it. She resisted my lesser self and asked more of me than I was naturally inclined to give. Once, when she caught me in a grandiose lie told to impress my classmates (about cooking a Thanksgiving turkey, of all things), Mrs. Tabor found a way to both make me come clean and save face. Day after day, she would not allow me to sulk and isolate; instead she coaxed and prodded me toward life. She was never harsh or cruel in her corrections; rather, she practically willed me to do the right thing. She wore black horn-rimmed glasses that for all I know were given to her by Superman, because she always saw right through me. It is not the memory of something heroic or spectacular she did that keeps Mr. Tabor alive in my memory in this, my fiftieth year. It was that she saw me. She got me. And she cared enough to reach past my developmental false start and play to my potential. And as she regarded me as worthwhile, so too did my classmates. There's a trick you don't see very often.

I did not notice at the time, but in retrospect, I suspect that Mrs. Tabor did not single me out for special care. She was the kind of teacher into whose classroom any parent would pray for their children to land. In my three remaining years at Chandler, Mrs. Tabor never let a week go by without asking how I was doing, waving to me in the halls. She let me know that although I was no longer in her class, I was still well within her sight. Then, one day she moved away, I vaguely remember, perhaps to Colorado.

The wisdom and nurture of Mrs. Tabor was not enough to stave off the effects on my adolescence of the undulating reverberations of the decade of social unrest. The changing landscape of the 1960s and '70s handicapped the social development of so many of us known as the baby boomers. All the old rules had been thrown out. We were just making it up as we went.

Some of it was just brutal. But as I clamored my way out of the culture of school into the life of a working girl, I believe some of the gumption in my steps was given to me by Mrs. Tabor. At every turn of accomplishment, I wanted to tell her "I did it." I wanted her to know that she was a planter of seeds. Thank you, Mrs. Tabor.

In 1999, my oldest child, Grace, entered the third-grade class of Miss Jan Stone. All three of my kids eventually made it to Miss Stone's third-grade class. And either by some cosmic coincidence or by divine plan, Miss Stone turned out to be the one special teacher in their elementary school years. Third grade is a big time in the developmental life of a child. I was twice blessed with an excellent third-grade teacher.

Keri Tombazian has been a radio personality in Southern California and voiceover artist for 30 years. She is the signature voice of the television talk show *The View*, can be heard on countless commercials, and has voiced promos for all the major networks. Keri's voice is heard in long-form programs including A&E Network's *Biography* "Lana Turner"; Animal Planet's *Meerkat Manor*; and the *E! True Hollywood Story* documentary series, covering Martha Stewart, Goldie Hawn/Kate Hudson, Marilyn Monroe, and Jane Fonda. She is celebrating 20 years of marriage and is mother to three teenaged children.

DIONNE **WARWICK**

Five-time Grammy Award–winning singer

Never Say "Can't"

Mrs. Daniels was my fourth-grade teacher and had a great dislike of the word "can't." As children we were constantly saying "I can't." One day in class I said "I can't" and Mrs. Daniels asked me to come to the blackboard and spell in capital letters the first four letters of the word *American*. She then asked me to put a dash before writing the next letter in capitals (AMER-I). Then she asked me to leave a space and finish spelling the word (AMER-I-CAN). She said the word as was written, expressing loudly the last four letters, I CAN, explaining that we were all AMER-I-CANs, not AMER-I-CAN'Ts.

The phrase "I can't" has been negated from my vocabulary since that day.

Dionne Warwick is an American Grammy Award–winning singer, actress, humanitarian, and activist. She is a United Nations Global Ambassador for the Food and Agriculture Organization and a former United States Ambassador of Health.

DANIEL GILBERT

Author, *Stumbling on Happiness*

The Back of the Room

In 1968, she was my fifth-grade teacher at Grove Elementary School in Northbrook, Illinois. One day I was staring out the window instead of paying attention when she called on me to answer a math problem. I couldn't. "What were you thinking about?" she asked, knowing full well that the answer was something other than fractions.

> **"One day I was staring out the window instead of paying attention when she called on me to answer a math problem."**

"Kangaroos," I said. She smiled. "Then why don't you go to the back of the room," which in those pre-Internet days was the place where we kept our precious World Book Encyclopedia, "and learn more about them?"

So I did. They are marsupials. Their young are called joeys. They live in Australia. They can box. Four decades later I still remember my kangaroo facts because Miss Leahy let me learn about them at precisely the moment that I most wanted to know. Rather than chastising me for failing to share her interest in fractions that afternoon, she encouraged me to explore my interest in kangaroos. That interest didn't last long, and I apparently returned to my seat in time to learn enough about fractions that I can do them today. But what I really learned that afternoon was more important than zoology or arithmetic. I learned that quenching a thirst for knowledge can be a powerful form of joy and that I could be thirsty about anything.

I never had another teacher like Miss Leahy. When I was 16, I was thirsty to know about the nature of mind, but my teachers were only offering facts about fossils and algebra. They were not pleased when they caught me staring out the window. They did not encourage me to find answers to the questions that intrigued me. So I dropped out of high school and began traveling the back roads of America, hitchhiking my way through the World Book to see what I could learn about memory, consciousness, attention, and thought. I became a writer, got a GED, went to college, went to graduate school, became a psychology professor at Harvard University, and wrote a best-selling book. I've had success and I've had adventure, and I have Miss Leahy to thank for both.

I actually tried to do that. But it seems that while I was in love with Miss Leahy, she was in love with someone else. She got married when I was in sixth grade, changed her name, and moved away. I've looked on the Internet, and once I even went to Grove Elementary to interrogate the staff, but nobody I know knows what became of her, and I never saw her again. I hope she's still teaching children that passion is their most important gift. I hope she has some inkling of what she did for me. I hope she knows that kangaroos eat grass and live to be three years old.

Daniel Gilbert is a professor of psychology at Harvard University and author of the best seller *Stumbling on Happiness.*

DR. WAVERLY **ELLSWORTH**

Retired physician

They Made All the Difference

I have always appreciated teachers for the very important yet often unheralded role they play in instruction, guiding, nurturing, and caring for their pupils of all ages and levels. I have been fortunate to have had many wonderful teachers and instructors, but two are special: one from very early in my life who not only kept me on the right path but undoubtedly kept me out of some really serious trouble; and the other who strongly influenced the way I practiced.

> **When I showed up in class with cuts and scrapes, Miss Standard asked me what happened, and then warned me in no uncertain terms that if I wasn't careful I could get into serious trouble.**

In fifth grade we moved to a new neighborhood. We were on welfare and living in a very poor mixed (white and black) neighborhood in Buffalo, New York. I was the oldest of four (later, six); my dad worked on the WPA and was gone by 7:00 A.M. My mom worked nights as a cleaning lady at an electric company and didn't get home until 9:00 A.M. It was my job to see that those going to school were washed, dressed, and fed and those too young for school were taken care of until my mom got home.

My mom had talked with my fifth-grade teacher, Miss Standard, a grandmotherly lady, about our circumstances and my duties at home; evidently she had said something about my wanting to be a doctor someday. I am certain this is why Miss Standard took a special interest in me. I was a member of a major gang in the area, having gained that distinction because I won a fight with the leader of the gang, who was three or four years older than me, after he had knocked me down and kicked me when we were playing ball.

When I showed up in class with cuts and scrapes, Miss Standard asked me what happened, and then warned me in no uncertain terms that if I wasn't careful I could get into serious trouble. Some children had already spent time in detention homes during the summer. Of course I didn't heed her advice and during fifth grade did get into trouble on several occasions. Nothing too serious at first, like being late for class, getting into some minor fights, not getting homework in on time—minor infractions. Each time, Miss Standard would strongly reprimand me and reiterate that sooner or later I could well get into more serious trouble that might keep me from ever becoming a doctor. I guess to punish me a bit, but mainly to help me, I am sure, she often kept me after class and had me do special lessons or reading. She would tell me I was one of her top students, and that this would help me later when I went to college—a million years away, as I saw it. Foolishly, I started skipping school once in a while; I was caught and ended up in the principal's office. Miss Standard was called in as well and told the principal and truant officer about my home situation, how much help I was there, that I was a very good student, and to this point had not done anything really bad. She concluded with "and you know he wants to be a doctor someday." I presume because of her testimony, I was put on probation. I really did well until about mid-spring when I thought my world would end. A buddy and I were out fooling around one night and decided to take a shortcut home through some yards when we saw police cars go by with lights flashing. We hid in some bushes until they were gone, but to our surprise the officers searched us out and arrested us. Unbeknownst to us, there had been a big robbery in that neighborhood, and someone had seen us go into this yard and called the police. We ended up spending the night in jail and had to appear before a judge in the morning. Of course my poor mother was there, all upset (my father wouldn't have anything to do with me), and I felt terrible. The judge accepted our explanation of why we were in that yard and let us go after an appropriate warning. He said he would have someone contact the school and explain why we had been absent. When Miss Standard found out about this she lectured me for at least an hour, telling me how disappointed she was. I was throwing my life away when I had such great potential; I was hurting not only myself but my family and especially my mother, who was so proud of me; she had really hoped I would someday be a doctor she could be proud of, but it certainly didn't look as though this was going to happen if I kept getting into trouble like this. By the time she was through with her lecture, I was near tears since she actually looked sad and when she said I could go, she simply walked away, without giving me the usual squeeze I had come to expect after we had talked.

All I could think about was how I had let her down, and let down my mother too. I vowed to change. I got a job as a delivery boy after school and though I remained part of the gang, I didn't hang out with them as much. Miss Standard sensed some change in me and again started talking about my becoming a doctor, asking what kind of doctor I thought I'd like to be, whether I'd thought about where I might want to go to college (here I was in the fifth grade), and encouraging me to get good grades because being on welfare I would need a scholarship to get into college. I finished the year without getting into any further trouble and pleased her by earning grades that were among the top in the class. Miss Standard even took me in to see the principal to tell her how well I had done. For the following three years I had different homeroom teachers, but I always made a point of stopping in to chat with Miss Standard. She always gave me words of encouragement and told me that maybe someday I would be her doctor. She is the only teacher I ever went back to see, even after finishing my first year of premed before going into the Navy. She remained as encouraging as ever.

After the war, and after finishing medical school, I went back to show her my medical degree, only to find the school boarded up and the neighborhood more run down than ever. I learned that she and the school principal had passed away. Thus ended that chapter of my life. I did contact some old friends and learned that eight of our gang had ended up doing hard jail time for stealing cars and other crimes; three went to jail for a long time for federal offenses. Thank you, Miss Standard.

Dr. William Mosenthal not only became my mentor, but he helped me make the crucial decision to go into thoracic-cardiovascular surgery. He was a superb general surgeon and one of my instructors at the Hitchcock Clinic, connected with Dartmouth College. He had completed his surgical training at Roosevelt Hospital in New York City. He had accepted the position at the Hitchcock Clinic at a very low pay scale, even though he had been offered a number of positions that paid far better. I asked him about this once, and he told me he never regretted his decision. He said he had a number of friends with New York practices, who made four and five times as much as he did, but most of them envied him, living in such a beautiful area away from the hectic life of a big city, and doing as many or more surgical procedures than they were. Being completely happy with where you are living, what you are doing, and what you can offer your family is all-important. While at Roosevelt Hospital he had been involved in setting up one of the earliest intensive care units in the country, and he did the same at the Hitchcock Clinic. When their new hospital was built, the intensive care unit was named after him. Years later, because of his influence, I was responsible for setting up the first intensive care unit in Washington State, at Deaconess Hospital in Spokane.

When I was about to complete my surgical residency at the Hitchcock, I was offered the opportunity to stay on as a junior staff member, which was not only an honor but also very tempting despite the low pay. I loved the area and the hospital. The clinic was part of the medical school's teaching staff, which was very appealing. But I was deeply in debt, I had three children and another on the way, and I was finally about to be finished with my actual training. Moreover, prior to this offer, I had decided I wanted to specialize in thoracic surgery because of my experience in Korea; I had applied for the thoracic surgery program at the University of Michigan, to which I was accepted. I agonized over this a great deal but Willie Mosenthal helped me make the correct decision by pointing out how far I had already come in my life considering my background, and that many other opportunities would be open to me once I finished my training, so I should not sell myself short at this point if thoracic surgery was what I really wanted. Upon finishing at Michigan two years later, I did indeed have many wonderful opportunities to join surgical groups and clinics with guaranteed income or to go to areas where the income opportunity was much greater than where I decided to go, but less desirable as a place to live. I chose Spokane, Washington, not only because there was opportunity there, but because it was very appealing as a great place to live and raise a family—and like Dr. Mosenthal I never regretted my decision. As a surgeon I have tried to emulate Dr. Mosenthal technically, ethically, and spiritually and have never forgotten something he once said after I had complimented him highly on a very difficult problem he had just handled: "I was once told you will meet surgeons who develop a real ego problem and who get to thinking they are God; but don't ever forget it is God who gave you the brains and talent to be what you are and all He expects is that you do the best you possibly can. When you do something great surgically you tend to be riding high, pat yourself on the back, and think how wonderful *you* are; and if something doesn't turn out the way you had expected, you can be very low and very hard on yourself and make all sorts of excuses; but you will have arrived at your peak when you know you have always done the best you could: your low will not be so low, your highs will not be so high. I think I've arrived." It is important to be your own person; but it is also important to have someone you admire and respect set a good example for you. For me, that person was Dr. William Mosenthal.

Dr. Waverly Ellsworth is a retired pulmonary physician and thoracic-cardiovascular surgeon.

GRAHAM **KERR**

Award-winning culinary author

From Darkness into Sunlight

I came to join Miss Dobson's class in 1945. I was 11 years old and "fresh" from the British public school. I had been beaten and verbally abused during my time in boarding school and was extremely unhappy. To step from such injustice into Miss Dobson's class was to go from pitch darkness into full sunlight.

The Rudolf Steiner method calls for an exam-free learning experience. There were no marks or grades and no position in class. The only punishment was to sit quietly with Miss Dobson and consider what might be the cause and effect of a poor action . . . and to decide for myself how I needed to change.

I played cricket and tennis without scoring and I met my wife, Treena, and fell in love at 11 years of age.

How good can it get?

Graham Kerr

Graham Kerr and his producer wife, Treena, created the world-famous *Galloping Gourmet* television series in the early 1970s. The Kerrs now work on lifestyle-related issues. Their focus is on converting habits that harm into resources that heal (www.doublebenefit.com).

BECKY **SELM**

Accountant and Web designer

Like a Fairytale Princess

It was the fall of 1969. Nancy Parrish was relatively new to teaching; her career had taken her to the rural community of Burns, Kansas. Miss Parrish was young and pretty, and of course *everyone* hoped they'd be placed in her class. It's not so much that we wanted youth or good looks—we were fourth-graders, after all. It was just that

> **ff Miss Parrish was young and pretty, and of course *everyone* hoped they'd be placed in her class. JJ**

we all had hopes that she would be a *nice* teacher, not yet wizened by years of, well, elementary school–aged children and their antics! Surely she wouldn't be a strict disciplinarian! She couldn't be!

Miss Parrish looked like a fairytale princess to nine-year-old Becky Vogelman, a fourth-grade student in her class. I looked up to her from the day she stepped into the classroom. She connected equally with boys and girls in the classroom, even though fourth-grade boys have completely different interests from fourth-grade girls. She was fair and respectful. She encouraged us to learn and she incorporated a lot of play into her lesson plans. And yes, she did manage to maintain discipline in the room despite being young and pretty! I don't ever remember being angry with Miss Parrish, only disappointed when I let her down. I remember wanting more than anything to please her, to gain her approval. She was that kind of teacher.

Miss Parrish took an active interest in her students. I liked her so much that I invited her to my Valentine's Day belated birthday party—and she came. She played all the party games with us as if she were ten years old, and she won the prize for being able to cut the most hearts out of a single sheet of paper. Her gift for winning was a paper doll book that she brought to school for recess. The following week she played paper dolls with us and she made sure that the boys had a new toy as well, so that they wouldn't feel left out.

One of my favorite things about Miss Parrish is that she allowed extra-credit assignments. We could mix and match the projects according to our interests. There was a folder at the front of the room for these projects. When we completed one, we simply popped it into the folder and waited for the credit. One day she announced a new program: extra credit for writing letters (longhand, as there were no PCs back then). We could write to our grandparents, our cousins, or anyone we wanted! *And we'd get credit for it!!*

I had wanted a pen pal ever since I'd learned to write, so I started firing off letters to any address I could find. I joined an international pen pal organization and was assigned pen pals in Northern Ireland and England. Corresponding internationally was big stuff in pre-Internet days. There was special airmail stationery, incredibly thin so as to be affordable to mail. I filled the extra-credit folder with letters until it bulged. From this extra-credit assignment, I learned more about other countries than I could have hoped to learn from a social studies textbook. I developed a global interest long before it became fashionable to do so, and from other pen pals I learned about life in Hawaii, Pennsylvania, California, and Washington. I also gained a lifelong friend in Seattle. In those innocent days, if you wrote a letter to a children's magazine that was chosen for publication, the editors would print your name, age, and complete address with your letter. I replied to one of those letters; the recipient responded; our friendship has now spanned 38 years, including many visits between our states, and now encompassing another generation of friendship and experiences. Miss Parrish gave me that wonderful gift, by encouraging me to complete that extra-credit assignment.

When Miss Parrish left Burns to go to her next teaching assignment, she asked us to write to her. She responded to my letters all through grade school, high school, and college. When I got married, I invited her to the wedding reception back in Burns, not thinking for a moment that she would actually come. Tears come to my eyes even now as I think back to seeing her open the door and walk into the room. My fourth-grade teacher, whom I had only known personally for one school year—my fourth-grade teacher whom I hadn't seen in 12 years—came to my wedding!

I can't explain where the time has gone but another 15 years have passed by. The letters have slowed down as I became busy raising young children, sometimes to the point of the annual or biannual Christmas card, but they still happen. I will never forget the impact Miss Parrish had on my life and my education. I will never forget the support she offered as I grew from a child to a parent. The writing skills she taught me as a nine-year-old have opened new doors for me many times in my adult life and in my hobby as a website designer. Miss Parrish invited us to explore new worlds, worlds that came to life for me, all the while continuing to be an extraordinary role model, proving time and again that she really cared about her students' education and success. She wanted the best for us, and she gave her best toward that effort. Many thanks to you, Miss Parrish!

Becky Selm is the office manager of a locally owned highway construction company in Salina, Kansas. She also owns and operates a home-based website design business. Married, she is the mother of two daughters attending college, one with aspirations of becoming an elementary education teacher and the other a graphic designer.

JOAN BAKER

Voice-over actress

Unforgettable

My fifth-grade year in school was by far the best year I had experienced since kindergarten. It was all because of my teacher, Mrs. Reamer. She was truly unforgettable. That style, that face, and that warm wonderful smile became my refuge after four years of educational turmoil.

> **My fifth grade year in school was by far the best year I had experienced since kindergarten. It was all because of my teacher, Mrs. Reamer.**

I grew up in Marin County as a biracial child in the early 1960s. Racism was still open and rampant and liberals were just beginning to figure out how to best position themselves for political correctness. The politics of race was in flux. Not much in the way of progressive viewpoints about racial sensitivity had filtered down to predominantly white schools like mine. Being biracial made the whole experience that much more psychedelic. I felt like I didn't fit in, even though I was unaware of my unique circumstance.

Biracialism was confusing and even frightening to adults. They didn't seem to know how to include me in the grand social scheme. The very few black people who lived nearby didn't accept me as black, and whites didn't accept me as white. And no one accepted "biracial" as a category. On top of that, I didn't know what it was about me that was creating this unspoken social peculiarity.

As a result, I was very wary of putting myself out there, while at the same time wanting to be liked by everyone. I was shy on one hand and very outgoing on the other. Naturally, this preoccupation with fitting in made it difficult for me to focus on school. My grades suffered and that brought me even more negative attention. In one case, my teacher literally sat me in the back of the classroom with a dunce cap on my head. I was crushed. Fortunately, I had a certain spunkiness that kept me fighting for my piece of happiness. Each year, I felt as if I had to start all over again, trying to win my teacher over—trying to prove I was capable, lovable, and worthy.

Enter Mrs. Reamer, my fifth-grade teacher. She greeted me with a smile every morning. She laughed at my jokes and loved to listen to my tales of woe. She treated me like I was her own—loved and adored.

Her approach to education was special. As a class we painted cardboard boxes (in 1960s pop-art style) and used them to partition a room and create our own personal reading lounge. There, in that space, Mrs. Reamer would gently encourage and guide us. By the fifth grade, I was gun-shy about reading aloud in front of others. God knows I didn't want to wear another dunce cap. Mrs. Reamer worked with me one-on-one in that private reading room until I developed my skills and courage. By the end of the school year, I could stand in front of the class and read without fear.

Unforgettable

I was so inspired by Mrs. Reamer that, at the end of the school year, I wanted to do something to show my appreciation. I had overheard a conversation she had with another teacher about her love of bike riding, so I started collecting money to buy her a ten-speed bike. I asked every student in our class to contribute money. Then my dad drove me to a bike store and helped me pick out a bright orange ten-speed bicycle.

I can still see the smile on her face as she rode her bike around the school yard while we kids screamed at the top of our lungs. But here's the clincher: I arrived late for school on the day her gift was presented, so Mrs. Reamer never learned that I was the mastermind behind her newfound happiness. She never got to know that I loved her for what she had given me. This missing link has troubled me ever since. It is only now, by having the opportunity to write this story, that I feel redeemed, by acknowledging all the Mrs. Reamers of the world: you possess a magical power in your roles as teachers, nurturers, givers of life. Unforgettable.

Joan Baker is a sound to be reckoned with, as one of New York's premier voice-over actors, for clients such as ESPN, Showtime, Chase Bank, American Express, ABC News, Lifetime, Lexus, and Disney, to name a few. Joan's also an accomplished actress, instructor, and author of *Secrets of Voice-Over Success: Top Voice-Over Actors Reveal How They Did It*. She also runs, with her husband, Rudy Gaskins, an award-winning ad agency called Push Creative.

Part Two

Middle School and High School

ROBERT ELMER

Young adult author, *HyperLinkz*

Dear Elmo

Picture the first day of eighth grade, when unsuspecting students filed into Mr. Edwin Little's English class. One look at his picture from that year's yearbook still reminds me of that sinking feeling. Because in a sea of smiling faces on the teacher page, his was the only frown—by far the sternest expression among the staff at Oak Grove Intermediate. His dark, piercing eyes and the pirate mustache kept us in line almost without a word. But that was only the beginning.

> **❝One look at his picture from that year's yearbook still reminds me of that sinking feeling. Because in a sea of smiling faces on the teacher page, his was the only frown—by far the sternest expression among the at Oak Grove Intermediate.❞**

I exaggerate only a little: between the endless book reports and the massive quantities of red ink Mr. Little scribbled on our papers, we nearly succumbed.

He did not tend to be shy with his comments and criticisms. That's how I remember it, anyway.

Beyond that, I recall best one small, scribbled comment in my eighth-grade yearbook (in red ink—I kid you not!).

"Dear Elmo," he wrote me on the last day of classes, next to his frowning mug shot on page five (Please note that "Elmo" is not my last name.). "It's been really great having you as a student. You have a fine mind and a great sense of humor."

So far, so good. Aside from the "Elmo" part, it sounded like something one might expect a teacher to say. But his final comment made me look twice:

"I'll expect to read (perhaps even teach) something of yours someday. Best always, Ed Little."

I read the comment over and over again, amazed, from the teacher I feared the most. He expected to read or teach something of mine, someday? Those words rang in my ears for decades to follow, as I worked my way through a variety of writing jobs . . . in newspapers, ad agencies, and finally when I began to write my own novels.

"Well, I don't know if I can do this," I could tell myself at those times I was ready to give up. "But Mr. Little knew what he was talking about. And if he expects to read or teach something of mine someday, maybe I can give it another try."

Beyond all the things I forgot in that English class, I remembered clearly the importance of a little encouragement, well-placed, in writing. As a wise man once put it,

"A word aptly spoken is like apples of gold in settings of silver." And so I learned first-hand the power of the written word to encourage, year after year.

Ultimately, that's what Mr. Little taught me.

Robert Elmer (www.RobertElmerBooks.com) has written more than 50 books for youth and adults, building on his experience as a news editor and reporter, advertising copywriter, technical writer, and assistant pastor. He's an editorial board member and mentor for the Jerry B. Jenkins Christian Writers Guild, and often speaks to young audiences across North America. Robert and his wife, Ronda, are the parents of three young adults and live in the panhandle of Idaho.

ROBERT **REICH**

Former U.S. secretary of labor under President Clinton

As Tall as I Would Ever Need to Be

At the age of 11 I entered Bill Javane's sixth grade. I was short, timid, anxious about almost everything a preadolescent can be anxious about. In the course of the following ten months my teacher opened my eyes to the world and to my own powers in that world, and in so doing he not only eased my anxieties and timidity but also allowed me to feel I was as tall as I would ever need to be. I recall him as a middle-aged man (in fact he might have been in his thirties) with a black mustache, curly black hair, a warm smile, and a playfulness that made everything he talked about in that classroom alive with possibility. On one occasion he pointed out the pretensions of white missionaries in sub-Saharan Africa

> **"At the age of 11 I entered Bill Javane's sixth grade. I was short, timid, anxious about almost everything a preadolescent can be anxious about. In the course of the following ten months my teacher opened my eyes to the world and to my own powers in that world. . . . "**

who tried to dress tribal women in cotton dresses that hid their breasts, only to return later to find the women still wearing the dresses but with large holes cut out so they could feed their babies and stay cool. On another he talked about why civilizations have needed to believe in God. On another he explained why scientific advances are usually little more than simpler explanations for new data. I remember him reading *Odysseus* to the class, and weeping at the call of the Sirens. I think I wept, too. Bill Javane turned teaching into an inspiration, and inspiration into imagination. Through him I could imagine myself as an adult—seeking to avoid pretension, seeking to believe in forces I could not explain, seeking to explain ever more elegantly what I could understand, seeking to be touched by the stories of eternity. And the adult I imagined became the adult I wanted to be.

Robert Reich is a politician, academic, writer, and political commentator. He served as the 22nd United States secretary of labor, serving under President Bill Clinton from 1993 to 1997. He is currently a professor at the University of California, Berkeley's Goldman School of Public Policy.

NORMA **VALLY**

Host, *Toolbelt Diva*, The Discovery Channel

My Height

In junior high I had an incredible growth spurt. I had always been one of the taller girls in school, but in seventh grade I shot up to become the tallest of the girls—and of the *boys*, for that matter. I felt like a gawky misfit.

To not stand out, I would hunch my shoulders, trying to appear shorter. My mom would reprimand me all the time: "Honey, you're going to grow like that! Do you really want to have a hunch in your back!?" "Please, your bones are still forming. Stand straight!"

One day, my class was standing in line, in order of size, to attend an assembly. My seventh-grade teacher, Mrs. Radeloff, walked all the way to the back of the line where I stood slouching my little heart out. She pulled me out of line and over to the side. *Oh, boy*, I thought, *I'm in trouble for something.* She said to me in a quiet voice something I've never forgotten: "Be proud of your height, Norma. You may not realize it now, but one day you'll be very happy to be tall."

With that, she exaggerated her already statuesque posture, smiled at me knowingly, and walked back to the head of the line.

Mrs. Radeloff was my biology teacher, but she was much more than that. She was one put-together lady! Her presence was unmistakable: She dressed with impeccable taste and style. Her hair and makeup were always flawless. She embodied poise and confidence. She was also over six feet tall. I never slouched again.

Norma Vally, widely known as the Toolbelt Diva, is a seasoned veteran of home improvement both on and off camera. Her media career boasts four seasons as host of Discovery Home Channel's Emmy Award–nominated series *Toolbelt Diva*, and of a radio show on Sirius Satellite; she is also a published author, columnist, and speaker, and is currently launching her own home improvement book series, Norma Vally's Fix-Ups: More Than 30 Projects for Every Skill Level (Wiley).

TERRY BERGESON

Former Washington State superintendent of Public Instruction

A Legend in Her Own Time

My favorite teacher was Ms. Hurst, who taught eighth-grade English at Barnstable Junior High School on Cape Cod. She was a legend in her own time, known by us to be the toughest, meanest English teacher in the world. She was brilliant and unrelenting in her expectations of our ability to read classic literature and think deeply and clearly about the meaning of the work. She had us write a weekly paper. I'll never forget the critique of my analysis of *A Tale of Two Cities*. I got a B+, which for her was a miracle. But when she wrote that I had learned—finally—to present a reasoned, thoughtful point of view, backed up with evidence from the text, I thought I'd died and gone to heaven. She was tough but she cared enough to challenge me like no other teacher in my life. I later became a junior high school English teacher and she was the reason.

Terry Bergeson is the former Washington State superintendent of Public Instruction.

KATE MYERS

Singer, *Blanket Sky*

She Knew My Passions

I have always had close relationships with teachers. I've been able to identify with them and learn a great deal from them. Really, I haven't had a teacher who I didn't appreciate and didn't feel like they helped me at some point in my life. There is one teacher, though, among all the others who will forever remain my mentor and my best friend. Denise Koebcke was my sixth-grade English and homeroom teacher. I was one of the lucky kids who had her for a three-hour block of time. Denise was always the "fun, cool" teacher, who all the kids loved and all the parents were grateful for. Denise and I immediately had a connection and, without warning, I deemed her my mentor. In our now-12-year relationship, there are so many special memories, I would never have enough time to describe them all. So I'll make this brief and to the point:

> **❝Any fear . . . be it simply asking a boyfriend if he wanted to go out with me or struggling through a deep depression . . . she walked through it with me. ❞**

Kate Myers

I would not be where I am today if Denise wasn't in my life. She inspired creation, nurtured my heart, expanded my mind, supported my passions, listened like a true champ, and gave even better advice. Any aspiration I had, she was equally excited about. Any fear . . . be it simply asking a boyfriend if he wanted to go out with me or struggling through a deep depression . . . she walked through it with me. When I think of all my friends, those I keep closest to my heart, most will never have the quality of life that Denise embodies. She is a rare gem, essential to my life. She is my voice of reason and my patience for understanding. She is sincere in her every movement and someone I wish everyone could have in their life. She would add that much more light, that much more radiance. You can only really talk about someone so much until you find that their awesomeness will never quite be captured in words: it's her presence that exudes life. We still talk very often and maintain our wonderful relationship. I know that anything I do in life, she will support and be proud of. Knowing that already makes it worth the while. And even though I tell her this, I'm sure I don't say it as often as I truly feel it: Thank you, Denise. Thank you for befriending me, thank you for sticking up for me, thank you for supporting me and loving me, thank you for being so wonderful.

Kate Myers is a singer whose mix of folk/rock guitar or melodic piano, along with a haunting voice, creates a sound that is quiet yet strong and moving. Her recently released third album is entitled *Instant Clarification*.

MARYA **HORNBACHER**

Author and Pulitzer Prize nominee, *Wasted: A Memoir of Anorexia and Bulimia*

Never Without His Hat

I don't think I've ever seen Driscoll without his hat. I'm sure he has a regular head under there, just like he must have a face beneath his beard; but I've never seen either, and likely never will. The man is attached to his hat. It's part of his character. He's a character in the story of my time at boarding school, where all the teachers only had last names—the others were Delp, Bozanic, Caszatt. Driscoll may be known as "Jack" to his friends, but that's of no concern to me. To me, he's Driscoll, baseball-capped, gray-bearded, and forever wearing jeans.

> **❝ But it was on Driscoll's wry, gruff watch that I actually learned to write, such as I can. No, he didn't teach me to write—he taught me to** *see.* **❞**

Jack Driscoll is a phenomenal novelist and poet, which I knew when I was shuffling into 8 A.M. workshop, half asleep in my blue uniform (okay, it may have been pajamas—the only rule was "wear blue") but didn't fully grasp until I was older. Figures; Driscoll had the poor luck to have me in his workshop when I was 15 and 16, and I was perhaps overmuch enamored of Plath at the time. But it was on Driscoll's wry, gruff watch that I actually learned to write, such as I can. No, he didn't teach me to write—he taught me to *see*. What I remember of Plath are the red tulips, the exact red that he made me suddenly see clear as day, when he read the poem aloud. It was in his workshop that I realized that I was in love not only with words but with images: the precise shimmer of the lake as a northern pike flipped and twisted out of it, the curve of the prow of a fishing boat cutting through the water at dawn. He's a Midwestern writer and made me realize I was one as well, and that the hard land, broad prairie, and thick woods where I'm from were subject enough to occupy me for a lifetime. The visible, tactile world had always consumed me, but I hadn't learned yet to put it into words; it was Driscoll who taught me to paint with my pen.

I remember the first time I truly understood how to write a poem: I was scowling at a piece of paper, trying to invent something pompous and inflated—what the hell do you write about when you're 15, 16?—and I suddenly in one mad dash wrote a poem called "In the Bra Department of Dayton's." I stared at it, horrified. What good was a poem about buying your first *bra*? Who cares? What does it matter, in the cosmic sense? It doesn't, of course. But it was *true*. Driscoll was always going on about the *emotional truth* of writing: he wanted your writing to be from the gut, real, honest, something that cut to the core. And this poem did. I could *feel* that it did. I handed it in and wandered out the door in a haze. I floated for days on the high from writing one true poem—it was a feeling I wanted to get again, and again, and again. When I got the poem back from Driscoll, it was almost invisible in the scramble of red pen—but at the end, there were his words, in the inimitable Driscoll block-lettered hand: GOOD POEM.

Never Without His Hat

If I had an in-house Driscoll now, I'd throw this blasted book I'm trying to write at his head and blame him for the whole endeavor. Best I can do is shoot him an e-mail, congratulate him on his retirement and on all the writers he's turned out over the years, tell him I miss him, and blame this whole endeavor on his hat.

Marya Hornbacher is the author of three books, including *Madness: A Bipolar Life*, and was the 1998 Pulitzer Prize nominee for nonfiction, for *Wasted: A Memoir of Anorexia and Bulimia*. She is currently at work on a new novel.

ALAN **DERSHOWITZ**

Lawyer, political commentator, and Harvard Law professor

He Thought I Was Smart

I was a terrible student through the first seven grades of elementary school. Even my parents lost faith in me, as evidenced by the following story. My elementary school had a three-track system. I was in the lowest track. When the school administered an IQ test and I got the highest score in the school, they moved me from the third track to the first track. My mother ran to school complaining that the test must

> **"Everything changed in the eighth grade when my teacher, Mr. Kein, called me in for a talk. He told me something nobody had ever told me before. He told me I was smart. "**

have been a mistake and that I could never compete with the smart kids in the first track. So they compromised and put me in the middle track, where I continued to get Cs in the academic subjects and Ds in conduct and discipline.

Everything changed in the eighth grade when my teacher, Mr. Kein, called me in for a talk. He told me something nobody had ever told me before. He told me I was smart. At first I thought he meant that I was a "smart aleck," which others had already told me, or a "wise guy," which was my reputation. But he really meant it. He insisted that my grades didn't reflect my intelligence and that I was underperforming. He recognized that I was restless and easily bored. Today I would probably be diagnosed with attention deficit disorder. To my Yiddish-speaking teachers I simply did not have *zits-fleish*, which literally means enough fat on my butt to allow me to sit for long periods of time. Whatever the reason, I was constantly squirming in class, looking at the clock and daydreaming about playing punchball, rooting for the Brooklyn Dodgers, flirting with the girls, or telling jokes.

Mr. Kein was the first teacher to recognize my potential and to treat me as if I had the intelligence to do well. He treated me as an intelligent student capable of dealing with the most complex issues, while recognizing that I was not highly motivated. He understood that it was his role to motivate me, and he did so by playing to my strengths. It worked—I did much better in the eighth grade than I had done earlier.

Then I got into high school, where my teachers continued to treat me as a failure. I did poorly in high school, except on competitive statewide examinations. When I won a New York state scholarship, despite my low grades, my principal suspected me of cheating until he checked to see who was sitting around me on the state scholarship exam and discovered that there were no good students in the area from whom I could have copied.

I made it to Brooklyn College by the skin of my teeth. Fortunately, they had an admission process that combined high school grades with test scores on a competitive exam, and I did well on the exam. When I got into college, Mr. Kein called me and reminded me that I was smart. I did well in college, and I am certain that I owe much of my academic success to my first teacher who told me I was smart.

Alan Dershowitz is a lawyer, jurist, and political commentator. At the age of 28 he became the youngest full professor at Harvard Law School.

TESS **GERRITSEN**

Author, *The Keepsake*

The Writer Inside Me

As an Asian American girl growing up in California, I faced powerful family and cultural pressure to pursue a "practical" career, so at the urging of my parents, I ended up going to medical school. Yet what I had really wanted to be, from a very young age, was a writer. And Miss Viletta Hutchinson, my tenth-grade English teacher, recognized the writer inside me. She nurtured me, she cornered my parents to praise my talent, and sometimes she pushed me up in front of the class to share my work. For years after I graduated, we continued to correspond. I left medicine and eventually did become a novelist. Every year, Miss Hutchinson would write to tell me how she liked my latest book. Every year I could expect her annual Christmas card, addressed to me in her spidery hand, detailing her latest adventures in retirement, the countries she'd visited, the plays she'd attended. Then one year, no Christmas card came, even though I had faithfully sent her one, as always. A few months later, I received a kind note from her cousin, telling me that Miss Hutchinson had passed away—and that she had never stopped talking about me, the student she'd always known would be a writer.

Tess Gerritsen is a *New York Times* best-selling author. She has won both the Nero Award and the RITA Award. Her books include *The Surgeon*, *Vanish*, *The Bone Garden,* and *The Keepsake.*

STEWART LEWIS

Author, singer, and songwriter

Changing the Face of Rock 'n' Roll

At a recent dinner, a friend asked me if I could name the Best Actor or Best Actress from the Oscars two years prior. Even though I consider myself pop culture-savvy, I was completely at a loss. Then he said, "Okay, now give me the name of a teacher who inspired you." Immediately, the name came out.

> **I remember walking into ninth-grade English class expecting to see a geeky old guy in a plaid shirt, shapeless pants, and brown orthopedic shoes. Instead, Mr. Potts looked like a hip older brother: curly hair shagged out, a silver bracelet, and boot-cut jeans (it was a casual Friday in 1985).**

"Mr. Potts."

"And he somehow changed your life, right?"

I thought about it for a second and then nodded.

"The power of teachers is overlooked and underestimated in so many ways," my friend said. "There is too much emphasis on celebrity."

Mr. Potts *was* a celebrity—to me. I remember walking into ninth-grade English class expecting to see a geeky old guy in a plaid shirt, shapeless pants, and brown orthopedic shoes. Instead, Mr. Potts looked like a hip older brother: curly hair shagged out, a silver bracelet, and boot-cut jeans (it was a casual Friday in 1985). As he told us about himself, his hands danced to the sound of the words, and his lively eyes locked onto each and every one of us.

When the class clown indirectly called him a hippie, Mr. Potts replied, "Better than a Republican," not missing a beat.

He handed out some books and had us each introduce ourselves, and then we went over the syllabus. At the end of the class he held up an album cover with a photograph of a man washed with light.

"One more thing. Your homework for this weekend is to go out and pick yourself up a copy of Peter Gabriel's new album, *So*. If you don't have the money, steal it." Some kids laughed.

"This album," he said with a sweep of his big hand, "will change the face of rock 'n' roll."

We all were dumbfounded, but we wrote it down.

That afternoon, my mother dragged me along to her aerobics class, a form of exercise that was very "in" at the time. I sat on the sidelines and gazed at the women, thankful that my mother didn't look like them: teased hair, cellulite thighs, and caked-on makeup. Mom was more au naturel, and it made me proud. As we were leaving I pulled her by the arm into Strawberries Music, explaining to her about my English assignment, and though skeptical, she complied. The clerk was just taking the records and tapes out of the boxes. He looked at me like I was a rock star for even knowing the album's name. I decided right then that Mr. Potts was super-cool.

That night after dinner I put the cassette into my Walkman and sat on my porch as the last bit of sun warmed the sloping hills behind our house. The opening track, "Red Rain," felt like a musical blanket, covering me in a dreamy soundscape that slowed my heart and tingled my feet. I couldn't take the headphones off; I just flipped the tape over and over again. The eighth track, "In Your Eyes," would soon become a No. 1 hit and the theme song to the classic Jon Cusack flick, *Say Anything*, a quintessential movie of my high school years from which I still can recite scenes from memory.

I took the Walkman into bed with me. When my mother peeked in to say good-night, she said, "Who is this teacher again?"

That Monday we all had our cassettes and albums in our backpacks, along with our notebooks. I didn't realize until much later the effect the music had on me—certainly more than a textbook ever would.

Mr. Potts asked us how we felt about the record. One kid said he thought it was "stupid," and another said it was "cool but I don't see what it has to do with English." I raised my hand and said what I had rehearsed on the bus ride to school: "dramatic and sensual." Some of the other kids looked at me funny, but I didn't care. When Mr. Potts said, "Now we're getting somewhere," I felt on top of the world.

I should tell you that all my life I had been playing music. My parents were in a bluegrass band and when I was five somebody threw me a tambourine. So I went on to play drums, and then guitar, and had even written a few songs. But they were folk songs. Until then my heroes had been Crosby, Stills, and Nash. This Peter Gabriel thing was a whole different story. Today my songs have been featured on TV and film, and distributed worldwide, and I have Mr. Potts to partly thank for that—not just because of that first assignment, but because he was the first person who instilled in me the power of possibility, the virtue of diversity, and the courage to step outside the lines that were drawn for me.

I began to look forward to his class. One day, when the lights were out in the room, I panicked, thinking he was absent, or there was a field trip I didn't know about. But when I entered, I saw a television set up and plastic bowls filled with popcorn. He told us that our next assignment was to write a paper on our reaction to the movie we were about to watch: *The Graduate*.

When I think back on it, Mr. Potts most likely wasn't allowed to show us a movie with such adult content, but he wasn't a man with borders. He was probably the type of teacher who had a stash of marijuana somewhere in his house for special occasions, or who had once followed the Grateful Dead, or maybe even toyed with bisexuality. Anyway, it wasn't *Caligula*.

I was fascinated by Anne Bancroft and loved the use of the Simon and Garfunkel songs, and though my paper was poorly edited, it had an unbridled passion that Mr. Potts took to. He gave me a B+.

Mr. Potts never seemed too phased about what anyone said about him. He seemed to take the good with the bad, and to try to learn from every situation. When a smart-ass challenged him, he challenged back. When an outcast ignored him, he figured out a way to get on that person's level. He'd make up games that everyone could get involved in, and it was in Mr. Potts's class that you found yourself making connections with students from groups you would never associate with outside those doors. He was a catalyst. But most importantly, he *cared*. Not just for his paycheck, which even as ninth-graders we knew wasn't much; his desire to influence us seemed inherent, something he was born to do. Leave a mark. And even the ones who refused to let him in still felt it.

Sophomore year I was captain of the tennis team and Mr. Potts was the assistant coach. Halfway through the season, the head coach became ill, so Mr.Potts took over. He was unpredictable and a bit silly, and, he worked us like crazy—on the court and in class. But it was worth it. He was someone whose trust and confidence you wanted to earn.

Since I was the captain, a lot of times I had to play Mr. Potts in singles during practice. Our levels were basically the same, although he was stronger than me and obviously had more experience. By the end of our sets I would be panting, my tongue hanging out like a golden retriever. He was so competitive; I had never fought as hard for anything as I did in those matches. It was always neck and neck, and he usually won. But once, at the end of the season, I beat him in a tiebreaker. Thinking back, he most likely let me win at the last moment, but at the time I was so proud I almost cried. And as he shook my hand I could have sworn I saw a glint of a tear in his own eye.

For my senior project I recorded a demo on a 4-track. I covered the song "After Midnight," and as all the teachers walked around to view the students' presentations,

I kept waiting for Mr. Potts. When he finally came, my heart did triplets as he put the headphones on and listened.

"Nice new take on a classic song," he said. "I like the syncopated guitar work. Good one, Captain."

At graduation he gave me a cigar and a mixed tape. I gave the cigar to my dad, but I would still be playing the mix if cassette players hadn't become obsolete.

I didn't see him again until about five years later. I was boarding a ferry to Martha's Vineyard and I heard a voice behind me say, "How's your tennis game keeping up?"

There was Mr. Potts, still tan and shaggy with a sparkle in his eye, as if no time had gone by.

"I'm a little rusty," I said.

I was traveling with some girls, and after catching up a bit, he said, "One of them your girlfriend?"

At that point, I had been gay for a couple of years, and comfortable around most of my friends, but not really out to my family. I had always been wary of that inevitable question, and the awkward remark that usually followed: a cast off, or a lie, or nothing at all, which only seemed to make it more obvious.

He looked at me and registered the apprehension in my eyes.

"Hey," he said and patted my shoulder, "I get it. I think I got it before you did."

I smiled and said, "Well, that was easy."

Later, during the boat ride, he came over to where I was and brought me a can of beer. We chatted about old times and once again, he made me feel like I was the center of the universe.

When we arrived, my friend asked me who "that guy" was. I didn't know whether to say "my teacher" or "my friend," and what came to me was, "He's one of those people that change your life."

Stewart Lewis is the author of the novels *Rockstarlet* and *Relative Stranger*, both from Alyson Books, and the upcoming novel for teens *You Have Seven Messages*. He is also an acclaimed singer-songwriter and performer. He lives in New York City and Western Massachusetts. For more information visit www.stewartlewis.com.

LEN BERMAN

Award-winning sports broadcaster

Saw Me Coming

Miss Sharon was my ninth-grade homeroom and French teacher at Junior High School 204 in Long Island City, New York. I arrived in ninth grade with a "reputation." These days a reputation might involve drugs or weapons. Way back then I probably talked too much in class. I had this "reputation" for a few years and had the feeling that teachers "saw me coming." Not Miss Sharon. She welcomed me with an open mind. She treated me as if I was the teacher's pet instead of a leper. I stayed late some days to help her with school chores and such. She was my favorite teacher, and I had a hunch she liked me too. She never prejudged me. I've never forgotten her.

At Stuyvesant High School I had an English teacher named Sterling Jensen. He told me I had a great voice and I should get it up from my stomach and learn how to project. He said I should be an actor! Up until then I had never thought about performing in any way. Thanks, Mr. Jensen. You were right about the voice part. I think he actually set me on the path I wound up following. But acting? Fuhgeddaboudit!

Len Berman is an award-winning sportscaster for NBC whose "Spanning the World" collection of unusual sports moments airs monthly on the *Today Show*. He is the longtime weeknight sportscaster for WNBC-TV in New York City. In addition he has written four books (three of them for kids).

GILLIAN **ANDERSON**

Actress, *The X-Files*

"Keep Going"

When I was in high school, I was a bit lost for a while. My grades were bad, my attention was worse, and my feelings about school in general were heading me in a southern direction. Enter a teacher named Sharon Babcock, who not only taught us English the way kids want to learn it—with an appreciation for words, an excitement for language, and a curiosity about literature—but also encouraged us to write creatively. The safe environment she created enabled me to write from my deepest places and, I have no doubt, helped me shed some of the angst that had been building during those complicated teenage years. A high point in my relationship with Ms. Babcock was when she visited me in in-house detention to help me with a poem I was struggling with. Not only did she show me that I was worth showing up for no matter what, but she liked what I wrote and encouraged me to keep going—keep going with my poetry and keep going in life. Her encouragement has stayed with me into adulthood and I still rely on it when I feel like giving up.

Gillian Anderson

Thank you, Ms. Babcock. And thank you, Bruce, for inspiring your wife to organize this book that led me to remember Ms. Babcock; but most of all, thank you for inspiring your classrooms. Whether your students appreciate you now or not, whether or not they look back in gratitude in years to come, the gift you have is that you can wake up every day with a clear conscience and know in your deepest places that you are doing the right thing. You are doing the right thing and you know you are doing the right thing and that's all that really matters. You can fill your heart with that.

Gillian Anderson is an award-winning film, television, and theater actress whose credits include the roles of Special Agent Dana Scully in Fox Television's long-running and critically acclaimed drama series *The X-Files*, ill-fated socialite Lily Bart in Terence Davies's masterful direction of *The House of Mirth*, and Lady Dedlock in the very successful BBC production of Charles Dickens's *Bleak House*.

FAYE KELLERMAN

New York Times best-selling author, *Mercedes Coffin*

In a Different Way

Even though I am a professional writer, I was a math major in high school.

One of the reasons for this was three of my high school math teachers whom I adored: Mr. Patton, Mr. Carrington, and Mr. Jacobs. Each touched me in a different way. Mr. Patton was a jokester, Mr. Carrington was a punster, and Mr. Jacobs was an obsessive-compulsive. His printing was neater than a typewriter's, but he was such a kind man and such a big influence that I began to try to emulate his printing. As a result, I had the neatest, most legible notes around. Everyone wanted to copy them.

I had a chance to see Mr. Jacobs again when I was given an award by my high school. I finally got a chance to tell him what a wonderful influence he was on me. All three were so kind to me at a time when I was at my most vulnerable. Not by being shrinky or overly attentive—just by being wonderful people. I could laugh with them and they spurred me on to a more meaningful experience. As a result I was a math major in college. Teachers don't realize the long-term effects they have on students. Mine taught me what it means for an outsider to care.

Faye Kellerman is a *New York Times* best-selling author of mystery novels. Her books include the Peter Decker/Rina Lazarus series, *The Quality of Mercy*, *Moon Music*, and *Straight into Darkness*. She has cowritten two novels with her husband, Jonathan Kellerman, and cowritten a young adult novel with her daughter, Aliza, entitled *Prism*.

JIM **BELUSHI**

Actor, *According to Jim*

A Mentor and a Friend

Our first meeting wasn't quite what I expected. The man with the shock of gray hair was swearing and throwing a hammer at the wall. He was building something, and one piece of wood just wouldn't fit. A high school student looking for the summer theater repertory program, I stood in the cafeteria staring at this mad carpenter. He was Richard Holgate, technical director of the College of DuPage, a two-year college in Glen Ellyn, Illinois.

> **I was a bit of a shoplifter in those days. I let it slip to Mr. Holgate that I was stealing tabs of butter in the school cafeteria. 'You know it's not about money for you—it's about getting some kind of thrill. You want a thrill? Run the lights for this show.'**

When I graduated from high school a year later, I enrolled at DuPage. By then, Mr. Holgate (I had only recently permitted myself to call him Richard) was head of the theater department. He made me his technical assistant. Bent on giving me a well-rounded theater background, he insisted

I stage-manage plays in which I wasn't playing a character. That meant building sets, with him at my side.

I was a bit of a shoplifter in those days. I let it slip to Mr. Holgate that I was stealing tabs of butter in the school cafeteria. "You know it's not about money for you—it's about getting some kind of thrill. You want a thrill? Run the lights for this show."

He never censored what he said. In faculty meetings, he'd freely respond to an idea he didn't like with, "Oh, that's a bunch of crap!" In his Film Is Literature class, we fought all the time. He was into Ingmar Bergman. I was into Rod Steiger's character in *On the Waterfront*. He would say, "Jim, you represent mediocrity." I found his honesty refreshing; he didn't want me to change my opinion as much as he wanted to push to recognize why I held it.

I joined the speech team, and Mr. Holgate helped me come up with a suit for competitions. On weekends, Mr. Holgate did remodeling jobs at the homes of DuPage teachers. Often I helped out. He never took a dime for the work. He'd say, "I know teachers. On their salaries, they can't afford remodeling." When people felt obligated to give him something, he'd say, "Give it to Jimmy." At one house, the owner pulled an old blue suit out of the basement. With the money I got from another homeowner, I bought a shirt and tie. My first speech took first place.

Mr. Holgate became a father figure, a mentor, and a friend. I loved my mom and dad, but they had very simple standards for my brother, John, and me: just don't be a bum. Richard Holgate made me work hard and held me accountable by teaching me to be serious about the things that really mattered to me. Those things turned out to be theater and film.

His agenda was always the same—he wanted to raise our standards in every way. We'd walk down the street, and he'd encourage me to pick up a bottle or scrap of paper and put it in the trash. Even today, when I'm walking my dog, I can't leave a piece of garbage on the sidewalk.

I went from DuPage to Southern Illinois University to study speech and theater and eventually joined the Second City Touring Company, where I became a professional actor. Mr. Holgate would come to my openings in Chicago, 30 miles from Glen Ellyn—which was really something, because he never traveled. I knew he was pleased with my performance if he looked at me and said, "That was fine."

Mr. Holgate is retired now and living in Manitowoc, Wisconsin. Although we no longer see each other much, when we do it's as if we'd seen each other yesterday.

He will make me sausages and serve them with good beer, and we'll sit in chairs he made himself and listen to his jazz collection and talk, sometimes for hours. Between visits, if I get a taste for sausages, he goes to his butcher and ships some to me. I try to send him money for them, but he won't hear of it.

The other day I was standing in the kitchen with my son Robert, who is 21. He was complaining, "You're always getting mad at me for not being serious." I said, "I don't care what it is, but it's time for you to get serious about something." Robert thinks I'm tough on him, but I just want him to find his passion in life and pursue it. That's what Mr. Holgate did for me.

Jim Belushi has been a favorite of film, television, and stage for more than 25 years, one of the great leading character actors equally at home in drama and comedy, and a gifted performer who can also hold a room as front man of his rhythm-and-blues band, The Sacred Hearts. His hit comedy series, *According to Jim,* just wrapped its eighth and final season. His best-selling book, *Real Men Don't Apologize*, was released in 2006. Jim also commits his time to charities and causes close to his heart, including the John Belushi Scholarship Fund, which services College of DuPage, where he met his inspirational teacher, Richard Holgate.

DAN **MILLMAN**

Author, *The Way of the Peaceful Warrior*

Forty Years Later

Quite an odd thing happened to me while I was deeply immersed in writing a recent book, *The Journeys of Socrates*. I had been writing for nearly a year and was nearly finished with the first draft when the thought came to me: *I should write to my high school English teacher, Mr. Thompson.*

I could still remember my first day in Mr. Thompson's class. I noticed that he had had surgery for a cleft upper lip and palate, and bore a scar, along with a difficulty articulating certain words. Yet he took great care to enunciate—a care that would carry over to all that he taught, all that he did.

"I credited him with igniting that spark in me that became a love of writing, and told him that he had certainly inspired—and changed the lives of—many students over his many years of teaching."

We studied Thornton Wilder's play *Our Town* and Nordhoff and Hall's *Mutiny on the Bounty*. That I recall these specific literary works after 40 years is a testament to Mr. Thompson's enthusiasm and power to draw us deeply into the history, drama, and humanity of such classic stories. He was also a Civil War buff and often hilarious raconteur, going into depth on subjects that others might gloss over.

But this is only the beginning of the story. Let's jump ahead 40 years. I had not thought of him in all that time, but here it was—this persistent urge to write him a letter. So I pushed away from the keyboard, picked up the phone, and called my old high school in Los Angeles, where I was informed that they didn't keep old records; I'd have to call the Board of Education. I did so, and explained to the person in Records that I wanted to write to Mr. Thompson, my tenth-grade English teacher.

"We have many Thompsons," she said. "What's his first name?"

"His first name? Ummm . . . *Mister?*" I half-joked before remembering that his first name was Irwin. I provided this information.

"Well, we can't give you private information," she finally told me, "but if you send the letter to him care of my office, I'll do my best to see that it gets forwarded."

So I wrote a brief letter, telling Mr. Thompson about my current career as an author, and expressing my deep appreciation to him for the guidance and inspiration. I credited him with igniting that spark in me that became a love of writing, and told him that he had certainly inspired—and changed the lives of—many students over his many years of teaching.

I had no idea whether the letter would reach him or if he were even still alive. But I sealed the letter, put it in the mail, and turned back to working on my book.

About three weeks later, I received a return letter in the mail. It wasn't from Mr. Thompson, but from his daughter, grown into a teacher herself. She wrote to tell me that her father, Irwin Thompson, had read my letter in bed just two days before he died. She wanted me to know that he cried when he read my words, and that they read the letter at his memorial soon after.

How could I have guessed that those few words, that simple impulse to contact him just before he died, might have made such an impact? I knew that many hundreds of other students had also been inspired and energized by his example and his teaching. Perhaps I had written for us all.

I hold teachers, and the life education they provide, in high regard. For years we had a poster on our wall that said, "What if the schools had all the money they needed and the government had to hold a bake sale to buy a bomber?" The service that teachers provide is as important as the work of surgeons or attorneys or engineers. What work is more important than serving as mentors to our children?

Each of us can recall one or two teachers who stand out in our memory, as Mr. Thompson stood out for me. Teachers who saw a potential in us that we did not yet see in ourselves; teachers who made loving demands on us to grow, learn, rise to the occasion.

It seems to me that we owe a debt of gratitude to all our teachers. It is a debt I can never fully repay, but that won't stop me from trying.

Dan Millman, a former world champion athlete, university coach, and college professor, is author of *Way of the Peaceful Warrior*, now a major motion picture. His fourteen books have inspired millions of readers in 29 languages. Dan also speaks worldwide. For more information, visit www.peacefulwarrior.com.

KEN **BURNS**

Director and producer of documentaries, *The Civil War*

My Friend and Teacher

My favorite teacher was a college professor named Jerome Liebling. He was my film and photography instructor, but he instilled in me so much more, giving me a sense of purpose, of mission. Though I graduated more than 30 years ago, he still is a friend and, more important, he is still my teacher, continuing to impart his critical message and vision to a now-aging student.

Ken Burns is a director and producer of documentary films including *The Civil War, Baseball, Jazz,* and *The War.* He has been nominated for two Academy Awards and won seven Emmy Awards.

BEAU **BRIDGES**

Actor, *The Fabulous Baker Boys*

Respect

One of my favorite teachers in high school was Clinton Dewitt Nye at Venice High School. His class was public speaking, but it was really a place where his students would talk about everything having to do with life. He had a great sense of humor. The first day of class he had a strange-looking doll he called "a nebbish" tacked on the ceiling. He asked us to think about what the doll represented and told us we would discuss it at the end of the year. And at the end of that year, he told us that to him it represented a strike against the establishment.

> **His class was public speaking, but it was really a place where his students would talk about everything having to do with life.**

When he gave us our final grades, he walked to each student's desk and wrote their grade in their report card. He gave my friend sitting in front of me an A. Then he gave me a C. My friend laughed, which prompted Mr. Nye to take my friend's report card back, and he crossed out the A and gave him a C. He then took my report card, crossed out the C, and gave me an A. I guess being respectful meant more to him than scholastic performance.

Beau Bridges is an actor/director, father, husband, and youth athletic coach. His movies include *The Fabulous Baker Boys, Max Payne,* and *Jerry McGuire.*

JACK O'CONNELL

Superintendent of Public Instruction, California

My Utmost Respect

I have two favorite teachers. They are Coach Dunn and Coach Holly. I always refer to them as Coach or Mister, to show them my utmost respect. After I received my teaching credential from California State University, Long Beach, I went back and taught high school at my alma mater; and Coaches Dunn and Holly were still there. They are more than just teachers; they are lifelong mentors and friends. Both Coach Dunn and Coach Holly came to see me be sworn into the California State Legislature and they sat in the front row when I was sworn in as state superintendent of Public Instruction. They have been present for me during the most significant events in my life. In fact Coach Dunn is the godfather of my daughter Jennifer.

> **❝In my case, both Coach Holly and Coach Dunn took extra time out for me. They were very patient, very nurturing, very encouraging, and very supportive. When a compliment was in order, I can remember them, as few as they might have been.❞**

In education, I like to talk about the three new R's—Rigor, Relevance, and Relationships. Rigor, so that we have a challenging curriculum; Relevance, so that there is applicability; and Relationships, which I have come to conclude is the most important of the three R's. It's about your relationships with your teachers and your coaches. In my case, both Coach Holly and Coach Dunn took extra time out for me. They were very patient, very nurturing, very encouraging, and very supportive. When a compliment was in order, I can remember them, as few as they might have been. When it was necessary to be critical, or to make a suggestion, they knew how to do that appropriately too. They are my two role models and, next to my dad, the most important men in my life.

My fondest memories with them were during our basketball practices. I witnessed from them a work ethic, preparation, dedication, and commitment that is rare. They gave me the work ethic that I have. They taught me how to prepare for success in basketball, college, and life.

Jack O'Connell is the current California state superintendent of Public Instruction, having been elected to the post in November 2002 and reelected on June 6, 2006. O'Connell previously served in the California State Senate as a Democrat representing the 18th District from 1994 to 2002.

ROY **FIRESTONE**

Emmy Award–winning sportscaster

A "Class Act"

Jay Jensen was my drama teacher in high school. I say "my" because everyone felt he was "theirs." Jay also "taught" men like actors Andy Garcia and Mickey Rourke, and director Brett Ratner.

He called himself "the teacher to the stars," but he was the biggest star. We didn't know it, because his private life was very guarded, but Jay was worth about $15 million. He worked two jobs, teaching drama to kids from all walks of life and taking us to perform at nursing homes and economically disadvantaged areas. He never said a word about the money.

He was a very eccentric man. There was a documentary made about him called, fittingly, "Class Act." Jay was a mentor, a friend, and my biggest fan.

In late 2006, Jay was diagnosed with prostate cancer. He fought hard, even making it to his film's Hollywood premiere. What I got from that film, and his life, was simple.

Money is important and God knows teachers don't see a lot of it. But working at your passion, sharing it, and passing on what you know and love to someone else is one of life's greatest deeds. It's more important than money.

Jay Jensen passed away in early 2007, and I owe so much to him.

Roy Firestone is a critically acclaimed broadcast journalist who has won seven Emmy Awards and seven Cable ACE Awards. He has interviewed more than 5,000 people, including nearly every major sports figure. Firestone performs his multimedia review before audiences in Las Vegas, at major sporting events, meetings, formal events, and conventions throughout the world.

ERIC LIEBETRAU

Managing editor and nonfiction editor, *Kirkus Reviews*

My Journey with Books

It's odd to think that my reading life began with the Smashing Pumpkins—my *adult* reading and writing life, that is, beyond Dr. Seuss, Hardy Boys adventures, Encyclopedia Brown mysteries, and *Calvin and Hobbes* collections. "Porcelina of the Vast Oceans," Billy Corgan's dreamlike portrait from the 1995 album *Mellon Collie and the Infinite Sadness*, proved to be the catalyst for one of the more memorable writing experiences of my life.

> **❝When I stepped into her class the first day of my sophomore year, I had no idea that this pleasant, ordinary-looking woman would be largely responsible for changing the way I viewed life and its connection to literature.❞**

As far as you take me, that's where I believe.
The realm of soft delusions, floating on the leaves.
On a distant shoreline, she waves her arms to me.
As all the thought police, are closing in for sleep.

That's how the dream opens, launching a journey of shimmering, magical images, and anthemic music. And that's where Mrs. Watkins, my tenth-grade English teacher, comes in, and where my journey with books and literature really took off.

When I stepped into her class the first day of my sophomore year, I had no idea that this pleasant, ordinary-looking woman would be largely responsible for changing the way I viewed life and its connection to literature. As part of her unit on Romanticism—that sprawling 18th-century artistic and literary movement personified, at least in literature, by William Blake, Samuel Taylor Coleridge, William Wordsworth, and others—Mrs. Watkins included an assignment that would pique the interest of nearly any 15-year-old mind: Choose a piece of music that embodies Romantic ideals, and explain.

As we delved deeper into the Romantic poets, I was particularly struck by Blake and Coleridge. Only later would I read Blake's masterpiece *The Marriage of Heaven and Hell*, but for the time being, I was enchanted by the muscular power of "The Tyger," the boundless adventure of "Rime of the Ancient Mariner," and the hallucinatory swirl of "Kubla Khan."

At the same time, I was discovering the transformative power of rock, especially Led Zeppelin. The day Mrs. Watkins assigned the Romanticism essay, I started combing through Zeppelin lyrics, many of which were inspired by ancient magic and fantastical elements in the vein of J. R. R. Tolkien. "Stairway to Heaven" seemed the obvious choice, but to a 15-year-old, far too cliché for my purposes. After rejecting "The Battle of Evermore," "Misty Mountain Hop," and "Over the Hills and Far Away," in addition to countless others I no longer recall, I decided that maybe Zeppelin wasn't the way to go—too dark, too overtly sexual, and, despite my newly found teen angst, perhaps too primal for a tenth-grade assignment.

Luckily, the Smashing Pumpkins released *Mellon Collie* in the fall of 1995, and I could tell on first listen that this album had at least one track I could defend as "Romantic" with a capital *R*—and there she was, Porcelina:

> *In the slipstream, of thoughtless thoughts*
> *The light of all that's good, the light of all that's true*
> *To the fringes gladly, I walk unadorned*
> *With gods and their creations*
> *With filth and disease*
> *Porcelina, she waits for me there*
> *With seashell hissing lullabyes*
> *And whispers fathomed deep inside my own*
> *Hidden thoughts and alibis*
> *My secret thoughts come alive*

It was all there: reverence of nature; elusive, ethereal imagery; the significance of intuition and feelings over rational thought; the pastoral as more important than the urban; Wordsworth's famous definition of good poetry as the "spontaneous overflow of personal." It even reflected much of the criticism leveled at Romanticism endured as being too dreamlike, too flowery. Corgan was known for occasionally floating off into the atmosphere; so were the Romantic poets. It was the connection I made between the two that demonstrated to me the power of both art forms—and the cross-pollination of thought that can result from using one to contextualize and analyze the other.

Fortunately, I got an A+ on my essay, but more importantly, that assignment truly sparked my love for the written word—reading it, writing it, analyzing it, and deconstructing it. Now, 13 years later, my fascination with music and literature has expanded exponentially.

Teachers constantly struggle to find methods to engage students in learning. Sometimes all it takes is a simple assignment that uses existing teenage interests as a tool to explore curriculum-based learning and beyond. I have Mrs. Watkins to thank for igniting that interest in me, an interest that informs nearly every aspect of my life today.

Eric Liebetrau is the managing editor and nonfiction editor of *Kirkus Reviews*, the premier prepublication book-review journal. His writing has appeared in *The New Yorker, San Francisco Chronicle, Boston Globe, Denver Post, Village Voice, Mother Jones, St. Petersburg Times*, and more.

GEORGE **M. DENNISON**

President of the University of Montana

Hog Heaven

I have fond memories of starting school almost 60 years ago. I started in a small, one-room school located in a little mining community about 30 miles west of Kalispell, Montana, called Hog Heaven, most of the way accessible only by gravel or dirt road. All eight grades studied in the same room, with a pot-barrel stove for heat in the winter, and every teacher I encountered

ff Those experiences made me think about teaching as a career, although no one in my family had ever gone to college. **JJ**

during those years was female and seemed very much like my mother. I enjoyed those teachers immensely, and they kept me on the right track of paying attention and learning. But their willingness to allow me to decide which class to become part of on a given day has stayed with me over the years, and I believe made a major difference in my life. They considered active involvement and engagement to be far more important than the formality of belonging to a given class because of age or some other largely irrelevant criterion. That responsiveness to my needs made school a wonderful place for me.

For the last half of the eighth grade, my family moved to Kila, Montana, some 20 miles down from the mountains and just 10 miles west of Kalispell. This school had two rooms, one for the first six grades and one for the seventh and eighth grades. As a student in the "Big Room," I experienced my first male teacher and I found it exciting and interesting. He took a strong interest in some of us, encouraging us not only to learn for ourselves, but to help the younger students. In fact, he allowed some of us in the eighth grade to help as teacher's aides. Those experiences made me think about teaching as a career, although no one in my family had ever gone to college.

For high school, I rode the bus from Kila to Kalispell every day, 20 miles round-trip, and became even more fascinated with teaching because of some outstanding teachers in Flathead County High School. Coming from a small, rural school, I found a high school of 1,000 students a little scary, but having wonderful friends with the same concerns helped me to do just fine. More importantly, I found the teachers quite willing to give me time and attention when I needed something. They also used every occasion to encourage me to pursue a career in education. Because of my desire to become a teacher, I paid attention to my classes, graduating 11th in my class. I wanted to make certain that I protected my options for the future.

When I graduated, I did not have the money to pay for college. My parents had other obligations, and the federal loans and scholarships now available did not exist. So I joined the U.S. Navy, served four years, and earned the GI Bill of Rights, which provided the support I needed to go to college. Still fascinated with teaching, I found some wonderful role models at the University of Montana. They encouraged me to work even harder, and I earned a teaching certificate to teach history and Spanish. Once again, the people made the difference. My adviser, an historian, simply refused to accept less than what he believed I could accomplish. The associate registrar of the university made me come in and discuss my grades after each term, and when I received less than an A, she suffered more than I did. Education had become my life because of the influence of teachers and other people in education.

After graduation I accepted a fellowship to graduate school in history, having decided to teach college, and earned a master's and then a doctoral degree. Throughout my years in school, I never forgot what started me on this course, the influence of wonderful teachers who instilled in me the determination to protect my options so that I could teach. I still enjoy teaching and working with young people, although I have served as a university president now for nearly 18 years.

George M. Dennison is the president of the University of Montana. He served in various academic and administrative roles at Western Michigan University, the Universities of Arkansas and Washington, and Colorado State University. Dennison received his bachelor's degree in 1962 and master's degree in 1963 from the University of Montana, and Ph.D. in history from the University of Washington in 1967. He and his wife have two children and seven grandchildren.

WAYNE FEDERMAN

Stand-up comic, actor, and, author

That Teacher

Philip Beasley, South Plantation High School: he was *that* teacher.

I spent two years in his class and, honestly, it didn't really matter what the course title read (for me, American history and psychology), Beasley was there to teach his students to think creatively. That was his mission.

Other teachers taught a curriculum—facts, words, theorems, skills. Beasley added a context—a framework for understanding. He always preached the power of dreams. He demonstrated how *everything* created or achieved by humans was once just a spark, an idea, be it the U.S. Constitution, a water park, the four-minute mile, or a hydrogen bomb.

"He was democracy personified. American History was first period; on the very first day, he asked the class what *we* thought the punishment should be for student tardiness. We debated and voted on it. The majority ruled."

Sure we learned of the Battle of the Bulge, of Pavlov's dog, but the primary lesson was the potential of your mind. Paul McCartney, he told us, composed the tune "Yesterday" in his sleep. Same with Keith Richards and the riff to "Satisfaction." Seriously—in their *sleep*. I never had a teacher like that before.

Every session fit neatly into his view. The founding fathers *dreamed* of living in a land without paying taxes to a king. That is how history was made. And, just as importantly, that is how your life, your history, will unfold, first, in your mind.

For extra credit in psychology he recommended we keep a "dream journal." He told us that we must begin writing the moment we woke up. Of course I liked to sleep as late as possible (I ran to school unshowered and without breakfast for years), so that was extra credit I never received. I completed a different Beasley project instead, the "treasure map," a collage of what you wanted your life to become. I pasted together a photomontage of Carlin, Berle, Lewis, Borge, Allen, Pryor, and a dozen other comedians performing onstage.

We were an undefined generation—stuck between the Vietnam-era baby boomers and the Gen Xers. The popular word to describe us was "apathetic." It was a concept that Beasley railed against. He would exploit any subject to spark a debate or provoke new concepts. Nothing was off limits.

Florida law required him to teach one semester of a mini-course, called Americanism Versus Communism. Beasley argued for the Reds—not because he leaned that way, but because he wanted us to be able to appreciate and articulate the benefits of a representative republic. It was important to him that we could be advocates.

That Teacher

He was democracy personified. American History was first period; on the very first day, he asked the class what *we* thought the punishment should be for student tardiness. We debated and voted on it. The majority ruled.

Beasley was tremendously encouraging (nurturing) of my artistic ambitions. Some of my earliest comedy bits were performed standing on top of his desk, in American History class. At the time I did a Kaufman-esque (Andy, not George S.) Elvis Presley impression. He allowed his classroom to become a comedy club—to help me.

Twenty-five years after graduation I went back to visit Beasley. I asked him if teaching had changed for him. Was the year-after-year Groundhog Day aspect of his job wearing him down? He said that it was different, that the majority of his time was now spent on discipline. Teaching was not as fun for him.

I'm not convinced we were any more disciplined. After all, Beasley was still a young man (27) when he taught us, brimming with new ideas and energy. Some days he walked us out of the building, across Peter's Road, and had class in the park—just to shake things up. Of course, I will always see him as that 27-year-old, with his mischievous grin and flop of brown hair. He was like Peck's bad boy.

I live my life as he once suggested: skeptical but never cynical. And 33 years later, in a very real way, I still stand on Philip Beasley's desk.

Wayne Federman is a comedian, writer, and actor. He is noted for his numerous stand-up comedy appearances in clubs and on television, his biography of basketball legend "Pistol" Pete Maravich, and his supporting comedic acting roles in *The X-Files*, *The Larry Sanders Show*, *Curb Your Enthusiasm*, *Legally Blonde*, *50 First Dates*, *The 40-Year-Old Virgin*, and *Step Brothers*. He currently lives in New York City and is the head monologue writer for *Late Night with Jimmy Fallon*.

HELEN **GURLEY BROWN**

Editor in chief, *Cosmopolitan* magazine

Not in the Right Neighborhood

Just let me tell you briefly about a teacher who seriously affected my life in my senior year of high school. Can I remember her name? Can I remember the name of the person who ran for vice president when Al Gore was elected president but lost the election because of the electoral college vote in Florida? No! Just let me say that this particular teacher encouraged me to write though I was only 16 years old. She perceived some modest talent. Of course I didn't get a book written and published until 26 years later but I know she helped (am feeling a little scruffy because I can't remember her name, but I surely remember her gift). The name of the high school was John H. Francis Polytechnic High School in Los Angeles, California, way downtown, not in the right neighborhood.

Helen Gurley Brown is an author, publisher, and businesswoman. She was editor in chief of *Cosmopolitan* magazine for 32 years. She is currently the international editor for all 59 international editions of *Cosmopolitan*.

JOHN H. RICHARDSON

Author, *My Father the Spy*

Diamond in the Rough

Two teachers made a big difference in my life. One was a high school English teacher at a Department of Defense school on the Yongsan military base in Korea, some-time around 1970 or 1971. I'm ashamed to say I don't remember her name. I do remember that the kids made fun of her because she was an odd and awkward woman even for a DOD school, which in those days seemed to be a haven for odd-balls who didn't fit into the real world.

> **She said I was a 'diamond in the rough,' a phrase that truly startled me. I wasn't sure what 'in the rough' meant, but it was the first time anybody had compared me to anything like a diamond.**

In my memory, she was very old-fashioned in her dress and a little bit musty, with a trembly and theatrical voice, a character out of a Dickens novel. The kids said she kept a flask in her handbag, which may have been true or may have been a teenager's way of explaining her oddness. I was not particularly friendly with her; I probably kept my distance, as suspicious of her as I was of other teachers. But one day she gave us an assignment to write a poem that started with "April is the cruelest month" and I tried to shock her with sexuality, turning April into a stripper who teased a man with seductive approaches and coy withdrawals. That was my shtick in those days. I wasn't surprised when she called me up to her desk, wrote something on my paper, and told me to take it to the school adviser. I left the classroom convinced that I was in trouble once again. But on the way, I opened the sheet and saw what she had written. She said I was a "diamond in the rough," a phrase that truly startled me. I wasn't sure what "in the rough" meant, but it was the first time anybody had compared me to anything like a diamond. I held on to that. At a time when nobody believed in me, it gave me the chance to dream of the person I might become.

The other teacher was Olga Matich, a professor of Russian literature at the University of Southern California. Olga was an unconventional teacher. She had a tangle of dark hair, she smoked in class, and she had a sardonic sense of humor. I can still see the light of amusement that would come into her eyes as she tapped her ashes onto the linoleum floor. Sometimes she held class in her apartment and served us wine. She had escaped Eastern Europe with a dying husband (a romantic detail that allowed me to weave a story around her). All of these things made it easier for me to bridge the gap caused by my eternal "problem with authority," as the counselors and psychologists put it. Olga didn't withhold herself or try to seem like she had it all together. She was another suffering human being, a little farther down the road. And she reached out. She selected me for a retreat up in the mountains that centered on the works of Boris Pasternak—a blissful weekend on a piney lake that included Russian scholars singing songs and drinking vodka. She hired me as a research assistant and paid me to read books by Russian philosophers. After a drunken episode when she should have fired me, she instead came to my apartment to check on my well-being. She attended plays that I wrote or directed. Looking back, I'm still touched and honored. Olga was this deep and rich and beautiful woman who was friends with famous poets like Joseph Brodsky and novelists like Vassily Aksyonov, and she cared about me. She believed in me. This did not solve my problems, but it certainly helped me endure them. And that made all the difference.

John H. Richardson is a writer-at-large at *Esquire* magazine. He has published three books: *The Viper's Club*, *In the Little World*, and *My Father the Spy*.

JOHN **GLENN**

Astronaut and U.S. senator

Ignited a Fire in Me

A teacher named Ellis Duitch made basic physics and its practical applications interesting to me. He taught me how a radio worked and gave me some tips when I decided to build a crystal radio.

Harford Steele taught civics. Mr. Steele was a barrel-chested man who prided himself on the strength of his grip. He carried around a sponge ball that he would squeeze in one hand and then the other. Later, when he became the high school principal and he gripped your shoulder to emphasize a point of discipline, you knew you'd been gripped. His civics course covered the fundamental institutions of the country, and he had a knack for making the whole thing come alive. He made history and government and politics into something really special. They were never remote, the way he taught them. You could see how individuals could exercise their beliefs and actually cause change and improvement. Citizenship in his terms was a dynamic practice. The idea that you really could make a difference stimulated me, partly because it reinforced what I had learned at home seeing my dad's participation on the school board. Mr. Steele's course ignited a fire in me that never did go out.

John Glenn

John Glenn is a former astronaut who became the third person and first American to orbit Earth. He began his career as a Marine Corps fighter pilot before joining NASA's Mercury program (NASA's original astronaut group). He orbited the earth aboard *Friendship 7* in 1962. In 1998, at the age of 77, he became the oldest person to fly in space and the only person to fly on both the first and the most recent U.S. space program (Mercury and Shuttle programs). He also served in the U.S. Senate from 1974 to 1999 as a Democrat representing the state of Ohio.

SHERRY LANSING

Former chairman and CEO of Paramount Pictures; president of Sherry Lansing Foundation

Unlimited Opportunities

I grew up in Chicago during the 1950s. While a student at the University of Chicago High School I took many math classes. On the first day of matrices class my teacher talked to us about how difficult math had been for him when he was young. It had been his most challenging subject. In fact he had once failed a math class before he came to love it. He wanted each of his students to be able to succeed and have that same thrill about math that he had. His

> **He wanted each of his students to be able to succeed and have that same thrill about math that he had. . . . This love for math is what pushed me to get my teaching certificate in math in college.**

belief was that each student should have as many chances as possible to succeed. He then explained that we would be allowed to take as long as we wanted during a test. If we didn't complete it during the class period that day, we could come by after class or before school the next morning to do so. He also said that if we still were uncertain about the subject matter and had not done well on the test we could take it again as many times as we liked, although the problems would be different. His philosophy was twofold. He believed that each student learns at a different pace. One student may "get" the material on Monday; while the next might not get it for two more weeks. He also knew the anxiety that some students go through while taking a test. Knowing that I could take the test as many times as necessary, I learned that there were unlimited opportunities in math. He taught me the love of math that I had hoped for. This love for math is what pushed me to get my teaching certificate in math in college.

Sherry Lansing is the former chairman and CEO of Paramount Pictures and the first woman to head a major studio. In 2001, she was named one of the 30 most powerful women in America by *Ladies Home Journal*. In 2005, she created *The Sherry Lansing Foundation*, which is dedicated to raising awareness and funds for cancer research and public education. In 2007, she received the Jean Hersholt Humanitarian Award at the 79th annual Academy Awards ceremony, in recognition of her work supporting cancer research.

BILL MOYERS

Bill Moyers' Journal, PBS

And So She Read

I do not understand the power of poetry to transfigure, but I remember the first time I experienced it. We had been studying composition in high school English, plowing through such necessary but rocky furrows as infinitives, genitives, and gerunds; the days were creaking by like turns of the torturer's rack. Then one morning Mrs. Hughes announced that we were changing course. We were going to study poetry. That is, she would read poems

> **❝ With her shoulders high and her back straight, and holding *The Oxford Book of English Verse* as far from her body as her arms would extend, she read. For the entire hour she read, until the bell rang and the spell was broken. ❞**

to us and we would listen, without commentary from her or questions from us. Inez Hughes could dissect a poem at ten paces with her eyes closed if she wished, but she insisted that poetry requires attention before it welcomes analysis.

So she read. Standing with her shoulders high and her back straight, and holding *The Oxford Book of English Verse* as far from her body as her arms would extend, she read. For the entire hour she read, until the bell rang and the spell was broken. She had a sonorous Southern voice, as versatile as a pipe organ, which rose half an octave as she read. Between her native drawl and an exactness of diction acquired in elocution courses back East, her sentences could flow like a languid stream or break, crisp and distinct, like twigs snapping underfoot.

She liked Blake. She agreed with Wordsworth. And she was haunted by Thomas Gray. She often read Gray's elegy, and as she did the poem took hold of me. Perhaps it was the rhythmic cadence: "The boast of heraldry, the pomp of pow'r." Or the romantic imagery: "Full many a flower is born to blush unseen." Or the stark reality: "The paths of glory lead but to the grave." Most certainly my teacher's voice left as much of an imprint on me as the poet's verse. Several years later, during my first visit to England, I heard her voice in my head the moment I espied the gravestones in the churchyard at Stoke Poges that Gray immortalized. Reaching the vista that seemed so unchanged from the poem's evocation of it, I shivered slightly. I felt as if I had been there before and was even now experiencing the setting and the emotion as Gray experienced them two centuries earlier. Only 22 at the time, I felt sadness at the transience of all life. Thomas Gray may have felt nothing of the sort, of course; it may just have been the voice in my head, but such is poetry's power that the emotions awakened then are just as real to me now.

I was hooked that day in class, and Mrs. Hughes knew it. She began inviting me to her home, where she would read poems aloud as I devoured the cookies that she offered me. Occasionally she would hand me the book and suggest I read. But my adolescent voice sounded more like a rusty accordion than a pipe organ, and after one or two poems, she would gracefully retrieve the book, pass more cookies, and read on, until the light drained from the window, only crumbs were left on the plate, and it was time to go. We continued these sessions practically every week through the winter.

Fortunately, Inez Hughes was one of four consecutive teachers—from my final two years in high school through the first two years in college—who believed in reading aloud to their students. Either widows or spinsters, they were married to the English language. Selma Brotze loved Shelley, Keats, and Byron (although, being a good Presbyterian, she never divulged if she knew about the latter's raging promiscuity; for her, the poet was a cracked vessel, the poem its delicious and unspoiled nectar, and it was important not to confuse the two). Mary Tom Osborne preferred Thackeray, Tennyson, and Shakespeare. Eva Joy McGiffin plumbed Chaucer, Milton, and the Brownings, especially the Brownings.

Bill Moyers began his journalism career at age 16 as a cub reporter. Since then he has won too many awards to count, including more than 30 Emmy Awards. In addition to broadcasting, Moyers was deputy director of the Peace Corps in the Kennedy Administration and special assistant to President Johnson from 1963 to 1967. He was a trustee of the Rockefeller Foundation for 12 years and has served as president of the Florence and John Schumann Foundation. He currently hosts *Bill Moyers' Journal* on PBS.

DEAN **KARNAZES**

2009 Ultramarathon Man

Thanks, Mom

I've always held a special place in my heart for teachers. Why? Because I was blessed with one of the greatest teachers in the world. She taught me about grammar and about sentence structure, but more importantly, she taught me about the virtues of service and helping others. Her lessons on history and geography were valuable, though it was her education on the grace of living that left its deepest impression. She shared my success and stuck by my side during my setbacks, which were often and many. Never did she pass judgment or convey doubt; quite the contrary, she trusted me more than I did myself. She could deliver a lesson plan with the best of them, yet she had the special gift of inspiring me to want to learn more, to care about the subject matter, to passionately embrace learning as a lifelong pursuit. Once, when I was facing the difficult challenge of preparing my college entrance essays, she told me to think with my head, but to write with my heart. I have since gone on to become a *New York Times* best-selling author, writing two books and having numerous stories and essays of mine printed in many noteworthy publications. I owe it all to her. Write with your heart, she told me. I will never forget those words. Thank you, Mrs. Karnazes. Thank you, Mom.

Dean Karnazes

Dean Karnazes is a renowned ultramarathoner and best-selling author. *Time* magazine ranked Dean as one of the "Top 100 Most Influential People in the World." Winner of the President's Council on Physical Fitness & Sports Community Leadership Award, he serves as a member of the California Senate Task Force on Youth Wellness.

TIM GREEN

ex-NFL/football player, *New York Times* best-selling author

Tolerance, Kindness, and Perseverance

My high school science teacher was also my wrestling coach. Every day after practice, he'd stay an hour late to work with me. My goal was to be a state champion. He made me that and taught me many other valuable lessons as well: tolerance, kindness, and perseverance. My teacher eventually became the first NFL teacher of the year (nominated by me as an Atlanta Falcons player). To this day I think of him often and call him every once in a while for some sage advice. I also want to say that I am incredibly proud that my own oldest son, a high school senior and captain of both the wrestling team and the football team, is planning to go to college next year to become a high school science teacher.

When people ask me if I hope my son becomes an NFL player or a writer or a lawyer or a TV personality, I say no. I can't think of a more rewarding and valuable occupation than being a teacher. I hope Bruce Holbert and other teachers realize their full worth. They deserve all of our praise and thanks.

Tim Green

Tim Green is a former linebacker and defensive end with the Atlanta Falcons, a commentator for National Public Radio, the former host of *A Current Affair* on Fox, and a best-selling author. His books include *American Outrage, The Dark Side of the Game,* and a memoir entitled *A Man and His Mother: An Adopted Son's Search.*

LOUIS **FERRANTE**

Motivational speaker and author

Unlocked His Advice

The teacher I learned most from in my life was my high school gym teacher. He was also my junior varsity football coach.

I was deaf to the rest of my teachers because I never believed I had anything to learn, and so I cheated, and paid people to do my homework, and did whatever it took to get passing grades. However, the lesson Stanley Aufieri taught me was that there are no shortcuts in life. At the beginning and end of every practice, he'd tell us that it didn't matter if we won or lost; what mattered was that we put 110 percent into everything we did.

One hundred twenty-five sophomores tried out for his team. Only 28 would make it. The odds were daunting, and I'd never played football before. But Stan Aufieri promised us at the start that he'd only pick the men with the most heart, and it didn't matter how talented we were. Well, I sucked; I dropped the ball time and again, even ran the wrong way, and I couldn't execute a play for the life of me, but I tried my heart out, and good to his word, I made his team.

I didn't play much during the season but that didn't matter. I learned much more than how to play football. I learned that if you put your heart and soul into something you'll be rewarded for your efforts. This is one of the greatest lessons I have learned in life, and Stanley Aufieri's voice came back to me in a dark and lonely prison cell, many years later, when I finally decided to heed his advice.

Louis Ferrante served eight and a half years in various maximum-security prisons after refusing to cooperate against former associates of the Gambino family. During his incarceration, he educated himself, becoming a writer. Ferrante's memoir, *Unlocked*, was published in 2008.

JIM BOHANNON

Radio talk show host, *The Jim Bohannon Show*

Drudgery Will Only Carry You So Far

One of the most dynamic teachers I ever had—indeed, one of the most dynamic people I've ever met—was Jerry Hoover, my band instructor for my senior year at Lebanon High School, Lebanon, Missouri. I'd been quite active in band, and was first chair trombone for five straight years. I had had good teachers before this, but Jerry Hoover was infectious in his love of music and his love of learning. It was his enthusiasm that was so important. Drudgery will only carry you so far into a lesson plan. Jerry could take a dreary day with clouds and rain and pump us up so that the 8:00 A.M. band period would keep us high till noon!

Jerry Hoover began at tiny Cabool, Missouri; went to Lebanon; then to a much bigger high school, Jefferson City, Missouri; and on to work with college bands at New Mexico State and Missouri State in Springfield, where he teaches to this day.

Jim Bohannon

If every teacher in this country had Jerry Hoover's desire, there would be far fewer educational problems.

Jim Bohannon is a talk show host with Westwood One Radio. Its *Jim Bohannon Show* of interviews and calls and *America in the Morning* newsmagazine are heard on more than 500 radio stations nationwide. Jim is a member of the Radio Hall of Fame and originator of National Freedom of Information Day.

PHIL MAHRE

Olympic Gold Medalist in skiing

He Reminded Me of My Father

The one teacher who influenced me the most reminded me of my father. Mr. Borck was my high school physical education teacher and football coach. He was a no-nonsense guy who didn't sugarcoat anything and told it like it was. He was very stern, yet a softy at heart. He rewarded kids for their effort, more than their talent. He was fair and just. Like my father, you knew where you stood with him. They both taught me that what one puts into life is what one receives from life.

Phil Mahre became one of the most successful alpine ski racers from America and was a major competitor on the World Cup skiing circuit from 1976 through 1984. Phil won a silver medal in the slalom at the 1980 Olympic Winter Games in Lake Placid, three overall World Cup titles, and a gold medal in the slalom event at the 1984 Winter Olympics in Sarajevo, Yugoslavia. Phil enjoys spending time with his wife, Holly, and their children, and encouraging them to pursue their dreams.

PATRICE **MUNSEL**

Opera star

Every Difference in My Life

When I first started out in the music world, I was lucky enough to meet a voice teacher by the name of William Herman. When my mother and I first came to New York to pursue my opera career I had a different teacher, who turned out to be a crook. I was ready to go back home when another opera singer from my hometown suggested that I get in touch with Mr. Herman.

> **❝He made every difference in my life and I am grateful that I was able to study with him.❞**

After listening to me sing, Mr. Herman told me he believed that with a lot of work I could indeed be the opera star that I wanted to be. I cannot tell you how much he taught me and how wonderful he was to a young singer out of Spokane, Washington. He gave me voice lessons several times a week and charged me a very small fee for them. He taught me vocal techniques and gave me physical tasks to build up my strength. He used to have me lie on the floor with large books on my abdomen and then had me sing a difficult aria while doing so. He also set up French and Italian lessons twice a week for me. My schedule was such that I spent five hours a day six days a week singing and studying the two languages.

My mother stayed in New York with me during my schooling. My father, a dentist, loved New York and came to visit us every few weeks.

At the end of two years of hard work I was able to perform nine French and Italian operas. At the age of 17 I auditioned and was chosen to perform at the Metropolitan Opera. I became the youngest opera singer ever to perform there, and Mr. Herman was the man who put it all together for me.

He told me what skills I would need for the stage, and he was a considerable influence of my life and career. Without his knowledge and help I don't think I would have learned as much or been as prepared as well when I eventually went to the Metropolitan Opera. He made every difference in my life and I am grateful that I was able to study with him.

Teachers are essential to the youth of America . . . or any country for that matter. They are the guiding light for young people and a good teacher can make every difference in the world. A bad teacher can destroy a child. To be a good teacher is to have the hand of God touch someone; the things that child learns will last a lifetime. There are not enough commendations given to this profession, I know, but those of us who have been fortunate enough to have a wonderful teacher will always treasure them.

Patrice Munsel was, at 18, the youngest singer to star at the Metropolitan Opera. For 15 years, she starred in many of the Met's greatest productions and because of these successes was featured on the covers of *Time* and *Life* magazines. Successful in all mediums—radio, concert, musical comedy, television, Broadway—she also starred in the film *Melba.* Her television series, *The Patrice Munsel Show,* was produced by her husband, Robert Schuler. His book, *The Diva and I*, is available on http://patricemunsel.com.

LEE GREENWOOD

Award-winning singer, "God Bless the USA"

The Final Piece of the Puzzle

Fred Cooper was my high school music teacher. He understood my talent, my passion, and my need to succeed, and he gave me every opportunity to do so. My family moved twice before settling down at Norte Del Rio High in North Sacramento, California, for my junior and senior years. I was already proficient on the saxophone and clarinet and was eager for more. Mr. Cooper expanded my knowledge of instruments by allowing me to try any instrument I wanted to learn, which turned out to include the flute, trombone, trumpet, tympani, and snare drum; I was the drum major for the marching band in my senior year. (Quite a feat as I was only 5 feet 7 inches at the time. Since then I've grown to a whopping 5 feet 8 inches.) As I progressed through my senior year Mr. Cooper prepared me for college by offering a new music class to only three students. It was Music Theory. Learning how to write and arrange music would be the final piece of the puzzle I needed to leave home at 17 and begin work in Nevada. I was offered a full scholarship to the College of the Pacific but I opted to leave home and begin my life's work. I also played the vibraphone, banjo, and ukulele, and finally the piano, which was my mother's instrument. Singing came along as well but it wasn't until I was 22 before it became the focus of my career.

Fred Cooper was a special teacher who understood his students and gave them choices that made sense to them. Often, we overlook our children's own desires and force our choices on them. Thanks to Mr. Cooper and my grandparents for letting me make my own choices.

Lee Greenwood is a country music artist. He has released more than 20 major-label albums and has charted more than 35 singles on the *Billboard* country music charts, although he is best known for his Top Ten crossover single "God Bless the USA."

DARRYL **WIMBERLEY**

Author, *The King of Colored Town*

A Man of Passion

I was introduced to Shakespeare my senior year at a rural and desperately poorly performing consolidated school in northwestern Florida. Lafayette County High School housed all students, grades 1 through 12, in an H-shaped bunker of concrete and jalousie windows built by the WPA sometime during the "Great" Depression. Our teacher for the 40 or so students who comprised the entire senior class came to us by a fluke: Lafayette County's consolidated school was, and still is, about five miles from the Suwannee River in the (very) small town of Mayo, Florida. There used to be two schools in the county, not

> **"At his own expense, our teacher purchased used paperbacks of three or four of Shakespeare's tragedies. Herbert Cumbie was willing to risk whatever subversion might occur with readings of *Macbeth* or *Julius Caesar* or *Othello* because he could not imagine young people claiming any degree of education who were not willing to wrestle with those works...."**

counting the segregated school in Colored Town, which was in those years, and still is, in some circles, easily discounted. The school other than Kerbo's was a whites-only school in Day, Florida, an even smaller burg just up the road from Mayo. DayTown's school burned to the ground weeks before I entered the seventh grade. The school's loss was terrible for its community to bear. The town of Day died on the day its school was reduced to embers. One of the hardest-hit members of that community was Reverend Herbert Cumbie. "Preacher" Cumbie, as he was locally known, was an ordained minister. Mr. Cumbie was also the principal at DayTown High School and its English teacher. A tall man with a high dome of a head and receding black hair. Sloping shoulders. Sloppy dresser. One of the first stories we heard about Mr. Cumbie was an account of how he had doused a blanket with water and rushed into Day's burning school to retrieve books from the fire-filled classrooms. He was reputed to be a man of passion. We all thought he must be just a little bit crazy. The citizens of Lafayette County could not afford to rebuild DayTown's school, even if they had been so inclined, and so all her students and most of the fallen school's excellent faculty were reshuffled without much ado to the fireproof, surviving school in Mayo; and so, in my seventh grade, the (white) populations of Day and Mayo were mixed. That was how Mr. Cumbie and his children came to us.

Mr. Cumbie was as near a paterfamilias as could be imagined in a Protestant and conservative Southern county. He guided us through *Silas Marner* and the Songs of Solomon with equal attention to detail. For a man so obviously hard on his son and his family, Mr. Cumbie showed great restraint in disciplining his class. Which is to say that he gave students their choice of punishments. He once let me take a paddling for Mike Tackett; I thought I was being cute. He wore my ass out. That combination of parts, by contemporary lights, would not seem a prepossessing choice for teaching literature of any kind, much less Shakespeare.

There were no texts for literature in our school that bore any hint of the Bard of Avon or his works. Nothing about Steinbeck, either, or Ray Bradbury, or Faulkner—a curious lapse for a school sweating in unair-conditioned rooms, in land that would be familiar to the Snopeses or any similar family. There was nothing on the shelves of our classroom to offend, but nothing to challenge either. Nothing, at any rate, that raised any serious questions involving the triumvirate of God, guns, and authority. But Mr. Cumbie had a rare gift, for a man otherwise ruled by absolutes: he was not afraid to challenge his own beliefs. At his own expense, our teacher purchased used paperbacks of three or four of Shakespeare's tragedies. Herbert Cumbie was willing to risk whatever subversion might occur with readings of *Macbeth* or *Julius Caesar* or *Othello* because he could not imagine young people claiming any degree of education who were not willing to wrestle with those works, to accept their hard assessments of the human condition, and pursue the questions ultimately raised. Not that Reverend Cumbie, with his hard-shell Baptist hermeneutic, was not willing to edit the Bard's unholy text: "To be or not to be" is not the whole question, Mr. Cumbie admonished us constantly. "The question is whether we are to be, or not to be, good for something."

Mr. Cumbie eventually located nearer to Mayo, to be more convenient to his new classroom. He pastored Airline Baptist Church, barely two miles from my homestead, and with his own hands built a house, which still stands today. He was a gunner on a destroyer in World War II. He drove a Comet, last I remember—he drove that small car as though he had a whip in hand, as if there were not time enough in the world to save every soul, educate every child, buck every bigoted idea or attitude that he was, constitutionally, unable to resist opposing.

He was a mad shepherd. Every girl and boy in Lafayette County's all-white school was important to this man's soul-seeking ministry. It was impossible to emerge from Preacher Cumbie's classroom unchanged or untouched. Within a few years boys would be changed to men in Southeast Asia. Mr. Cumbie, a Navy veteran himself from the Second World War, was never a cheerleader for that expedition. He spoke from the pulpit candidly, and more obliquely in the classroom, warning that *dulce et decorum est pro patria mori*. He was a hard father, I am sure, an impassioned educator, and a preacher.

Mr. Cumbie died, with his wife, driving too fast on a return trip from some revival in Alabama. His orphaned children were taken in by a neighboring family. His son would stand beside me at our high school graduation. A fire brought us Mr. Cumbie. A fire would take him away, but not so far that his own burning heat cannot still be felt.

Darryl Wimberley was born in St. Augustine, Florida. His works include A *Rock and a Hard Place*, *Dead Man's Bay*, *Strawman's Hammock*, *Pepperfish Keys*, *A Tinker's Damn*, and *The King of Colored Town*, which was awarded the Willie Morris Prize for Southern Fiction in 2008. Darryl writes full-time in Austin, Texas. He is married and has two children.

NICK **TAYLOR**

Author, *American-Made*

Serious Business

I wouldn't say Frank Riley was my favorite teacher, but he was the best I ever had, and the one I remember best, so I guess that amounts to the same thing. I don't recall if I was a junior or a senior at Fort Myers Senior High in Fort Myers, Florida, when I first entered Mr. Riley's classroom for his course in English composition. I had

> **❝I wouldn't say Frank Riley was my favorite teacher, but he was the best I ever had, and the one I remember best, so I guess that amounts to the same thing. ❞**

always been interested in writing and thought I was pretty good at it. But I had never thought of it as a discipline. That changed in Mr. Riley's class.

He was a skinny guy who had a slump and walked with his hips thrust forward. Pacing before the blackboard in his classroom, he looked like a cartoonist had used a hollow new moon to model him. He had a habit of clapping his hands to the sides of his head and pushing his hair back when we were slow to grasp a point he was trying to convey. He would widen his eyes in amazement that we were so obtuse. He wanted us to know that writing was serious business.

The discipline of writing consisted of simple, declarative sentences. The active voice almost always trumped the passive. Qualifiers—"perhaps," "a bit," "rather"—muddied the waters. Adjectives and adverbs could be useful, but usually weren't if you had chosen the right noun or verb. All of this, for me, lifted writing out of a morass of sloppiness and gave it new vigor.

Mr. Riley had a lot of energy, and he was fierce. He demanded attention. The kids in our college preparatory class were pretty smart, and some were inclined to skate. Notes passed back and forth; kids read magazines behind their upraised notebooks. That all stopped, however, the day Mr. Riley got irritated by one of our cheekier classmates, who kept whispering to the kid across the aisle. After repeated warnings, Mr. R. picked up an eraser from the blackboard and hurled it at the boy. The eraser caromed off a wall and sent up a cloud of chalk dust that settled in the silence as we all held our breaths. Mr. Riley glared at the offender and brushed his hands, sending up more chalk dust. Then he looked around the room at the rest of us. The message could not have been clearer.

In composition, obviously, we were graded mostly on essays and other writing. I don't remember any of my subjects, but I do remember that Mr. Riley's comments were clear and unsparing, not harsh but, rather, helpful. He aimed to instruct more than to criticize. He was the same as the director of my senior class play, in which I played the ghost of a Revolutionary War soldier haunting a house in New York's Gramercy Park and complicating its mistress's romantic life.

Mr. Riley's clear direction didn't lead me to the stage, but it helped me enormously in writing, the career I did pursue. After 11 books on my own and in collaboration, and many more articles than I can count, I use his lessons every day and will never stop being grateful for his skill and commitment as a teacher and ultimately, I think, his friendship.

Nick Taylor is a critically acclaimed author whose most recent book is *American-Made: The Enduring Legacy of the WPA*. His others include *Sins of the Father, Laser, A Necessary End,* and *Bass Wars*. He also collaborated with John Glenn on *John Glenn: A Memoir,* which was a *New York Times* best seller.

KEITH **JACKSON**

Sportscaster for over 50 years, ABC

You'll Never Amount to a Hill of Beans

Graduating from a little country high school in West Georgia in 1946, I was determined to join the U.S. Marines as quickly as possible. All my family had been Marines going back to the 1920s and though the big war was over, I wanted to go. In those days, there were only 11 grades; leaving a graduating class of 28 students, off I went. I fibbed a little, about four months' worth, and was accepted. Guess they were happy to find some eager young pups after the long struggle of World War II.

On my departure, one of my favorite teachers, Ms. Mary Baxter, hammered me and my decision and left me with these cutting words: "If you go into the Marines, you will never amount to a hill of beans and you'll probably get killed." That was a Southern lady talking, mind you! Those words still ring in my ears more than six decades later, especially when I'm in a challenging moment. And I've had many of those, having traveled across 33 countries and I don't know how many millions of miles. Doesn't matter! What mattered was the challenge that little woman teacher threw at me from the steps of that old redbrick schoolhouse when I was 16 and thought I was bulletproof. The teacher almost never knows which fingerprint will have the most meaning for those who have gone . . . but bless 'em for keeping on.

If I ever chance to see Miss Mary again, I will be happy to tell her that in my 54 years of professional life I had two jobs and one great and glorious wife and three children. Which clearly proves I don't know a damned thing about show business.

Keith Jackson is a former sportscaster, known for his long career with ABC Sports television; his coverage of college football; his style of folksy, down-to-earth commentary and deep voice; and for coining the lines "Whoa, Nellie!" and "Fum-BLE!"

ROBERT **PINSKY**

Poet Laureate

Unquestioned Authority

With unquestioned authority Mr. Angus MacWithey taught woodshop and mechanical drawing to unruly adolescent boys, including the Bad Class, as our group was called. He never raised his voice or made a threat. However, he wielded a lethal, pale blue stare of disapproval, supported by a samurai carriage of his body.

> **With unquestioned authority Mr. Angus MacWithey taught woodshop and mechanical drawing to unruly adolescent boys. . . . He never raised his voice or made a threat. However, he wielded a lethal, pale blue stare of disapproval, supported by a samurai carriage of his body.**

He led us would-be thugs into the first intellectual discussion I can remember. How do you determine the front of an object? he asked.

Um, if it moved, the side that would go first? (Then which side of a factory would that be?) The largest side? (Then which side of a cube would that be?) The part where something comes in or out? (So the front of a toilet is from below, or above? Or is the front of your car where the doors are? Or the trunk?) We reasoned and theorized for a session of some length. Juvenile-delinquent philosophers, Aristotelian hoodlums. So Mr. MacWithey taught us the nature of definition.

He also taught analogical thinking. A ripsaw can be distinguished from a crosscut because the rip teeth have the shape made by the upright and leg of the letter *R*.

I brought him my drawing, the dimension lines and drawing lines executed with distinguishing degrees of pressure, laboriously, as he told us to do. Something's missing, he said. What, Mr. Mac? Gently he tapped my head, then his. I had forgotten the arrowheads on the dimension lines.

An arrowhead, he taught us, is not a graceless *V* plunked at the tip of a dimension line like two ribs of a broken umbrella teetering on its handle. The twin barbs of an arrowhead should curve gracefully away from the dimension line's tip, like water dividing away from the point of a boat's prow. So he taught the significance of formal beauty, and its traditions, as well.

Once he ordered me to tell the class my semester grade: "A." He commended me to the other little brutes: someone with not much talent who had worked hard. (In English, social studies, mathematics, I was getting Ds and Cs, an occasional F.) He taught me to value work, and to understand that I was capable of work. He respected his material and he respected us: on principle and because that was his work.

(The front of an object is the view that gives the most information about it.)

Robert Pinsky is a poet, essayist, literary critic, and translator. From 1997 to 2000, he served as Poet Laureate Consultant in Poetry to the Library of Congress. Pinsky is the author of many books, most recently *Gulf Music* (poetry) and *Thousands of Broadways* (prose).

KIM **ALEXIS**

Supermodel

Break Me or Make Me Smarter

I remember a high school teacher who had a big impact on me. He pushed me. Too hard at the time but now I see that he was either going to break me or make me stronger.

His name was John Koplas. He knew what I could do and did not give up on me when I wanted to "coast" through senior high.

Kim Alexis quickly made her mark in the modeling industry, earning a stint as a Revlon spokesperson, doing countless TV and print ads, and gracing the cover of over 500 magazines, as well as six appearances in the coveted *Sports Illustrated* swimsuit issues.

BERNARD **CORNWELL**

Author, *Sharpe's Story*

"Read It," He Said

His name, an unfortunate name for a teacher, was Dick Hole. I did not make that up. He was really Richard Hole, but to everyone at my school he was Dick, a nickname that did no justice to his formidable presence. He taught English, and my abiding memory is of a tall, thin, aquiline man swathed in a faded black scholar's gown. He was arrogant and civilized, bitingly sarcastic, frighteningly well read, intolerant, condescending, aloof, bored, awesome, and, of course, inspiring. Dick Hole

> **❝ 'Read it,' he had said, and said nothing more. It was *The Warden*, by Anthony Trollope, and I have no idea why he selected me for that book, but the match was perfect; every couple of weeks he would give me another book. ❞**

understood that we had to climb to his level of sophistication; he did not believe in stooping to our level. The aspiration of a child, after all, should be to grow up.

The school, the equivalent of an American high school, was a boys-only boarding school set in the bucolic landscape of the English West Country. It was a private school and knew only too well that adolescent boys must be kept busy, so inflicted rugby, cricket, field hockey, and rowing on us, insisted we took a cold bath every morning before worshipping a muscular God in the school chapel, and imposed a taxing academic regime which, in the manner of English secondary education, allowed us to specialize early. I chose English and history as my subjects, and Dick Hole, I recall, groaned slightly when I told him I would be in the equivalent of his 11th-grade class. "I suppose I have small choice," I think he murmured.

Yet he had nurtured me. Four years earlier he had held me back as I left his classroom and thrust a book into my hand. "Read it," he had said, and said nothing more. It was *The Warden*, by Anthony Trollope, and I have no idea why he selected me for that book, but the match was perfect; every couple of weeks he would give me another book. He never inquired if I had read the previous one let alone condescended to discuss it. In class we studied Chaucer and Shakespeare, Wordsworth and Tennyson, yet he was giving me an alternative curriculum that took me from Trollope to John Cowper Powys (still a passion) and on to what were then the "moderns": Yeats, Eliot, Pound, and Gerard Manley Hopkins.

The most unlikely thing about Dick Hole was his choice of car, a Triumph TR2. It was a sports car built for two and I remember him stopping beside me once, some five miles from the school, and offering me a ride. It was starting to rain and he had a passenger. "Climb on," he said in his lordly fashion, waving at the luggage rack mounted on the boot. I climbed on. Today, of course, he would be condemned for endangering a life, but I still remember that wild, exhilarating ride through twisting country lanes, clinging onto the chrome rack for dear life, and laughing for the sheer joy of the experience.

"Read It," He Said

In the 12th grade I was expelled from the school for showing too much interest in girls (the school is coed now, so I suppose the interest is tolerated) and never saw Dick Hole again, though he did write me a note. "You were not a complete waste of my time," the note said, and I still wish it were true.

Bernard Cornwell is an English author of historical novels. He is best known for his novels about Napoleonic Wars rifleman Richard Sharpe, which were adapted into a series of Sharpe television films.

LORD **JEFFREY ARCHER**

Author and politician

Fortunate Children

"Archer, your latest attempt at an essay only proves that relevance is the refuge of the inhibited."

When reading this, you might find it sarcastic, even cynical, but when spoken by Alan Quilter the words were delivered with humor and affection.

His passion for the Bard, and of every other writer from Ian Fleming to Proust, and his desire to impart that passion to those who lounged in his classroom on lazy summer afternoons, never dwindled. When the bell struck 5 o'clock and other teachers departed for what they considered the end of a day's work, he could be found in the winter on the rugby pitch refereeing, and in the summer on the square, umpiring. Not for him the glory of the First XV or the First X1, but the Under-14 Thirds, where he had to tolerate me once again.

Alan went on to be headmaster of Wells Cathedral School (1964–1986), and the vast turnout for his funeral was testimony to the fact that generations of fortunate children were inflicted with his passions. I miss him.

Lord Jeffrey Archer

Lord Jeffrey Archer is an author, charity auctioneer, politician, and art collector. Lord Archer has sold over 200 million books worldwide. He has served five years in the House of Commons and 17 years in the House of Lords. He ran the 100 yards for Great Britain in 1966 and completed the London Marathon considerably more slowly in 2004—being overtaken by a pillar-box.

ANN TURNER

Children's and young adult author

She Believed in Me

Mrs. Belk strode into the science classroom, short red hair swinging. After a quick but measured glance around the room, it was clear that this was a woman of high expectations. She would not tolerate shoddy work, tardiness, or anything less than our best. But even more than this, Mrs. Belk was one of the first teachers in high school who believed in my intelligence and capacities. It was she who told my parent during a parent/teacher conference, "Ann could be getting all As if she wanted to."

Mom repeated that to me, with a proud but slightly disbelieving smile, even

> **On a hike into the woods to examine plant life, Mrs. Belk invited our biology class to her house. . . . I thought it most romantic, and this opinion was strengthened when she introduced us to her husband, a writer, who was at home, sitting on a couch with a yellow notepad in front of him. I did not know of one man who stayed home during the working day, and this added to Mrs. Belk's cachet.**

though I had always done well in school. The standard-bearer of the family's intelligence was my older brother, on whose shoulders the burden of earning academic achievements rested (he was a National Merit Scholar and an intensely bright boy). But despite my brother's stellar record, Mrs. Belk believed in and supported me, as I studied science with her for the next four years in our small, rural high school.

Sometimes the questions we ask can be more earth-shattering than their answers. In one class, where Mrs. Belk was teaching about equal and opposite reactions and how the boards under one's feet would exert a force back at us when we walked on them, I was seized with inspiration: "Is the force there in the boards, Mrs. Belk, even when we aren't walking on them?" I do not remember her words, simply her grin of surprise and delight at my question. I think the freedom to ask questions in her class has continued to be a part of my character, as I question so much about my life, culture, and world. In biology, I remember cutting open the seed-bearing part of the green plant and examining it under a microscope. The minute white seeds glistened, ready for new beginnings. At my cry of amazement, Mrs. Belk came over to share in my wonder, as if it were the first time she, too, had seen the possibilities of new life.

On a hike into the woods to examine plant life, Mrs. Belk invited our biology class to her house—a small cabin nestled at the base of a huge rock slab. I thought it most romantic, and this opinion was strengthened when she introduced us to her husband, a writer, who was at home, sitting on a couch with a yellow notepad in front of him. I did not know of one man who stayed home during the working day, and this added to

Mrs. Belk's cachet. Someone willing to buck convention and ordinary life would live with a writer.

In my senior year, Mrs. Belk taught physics. For a student who was deeply suspicious of and uneasy with math, she made the subject fascinating and accessible. One day she brought in her record player and played one of Bach's Brandenburg Concertos to illustrate the mathematical precision of his music. I'm not sure if this tied in with wave theory or not; I just remember the lively notes floating out over the hot classroom, a respite and inspiration during our day.

Even better than believing in me and sharing with me the wonder of science, Mrs. Belk strongly recommended I apply to Bates College, her alma mater. I did, was accepted, and learned that Mrs. Belk's old English professor (and I do mean old) was still teaching at the college. Somehow, my life became even more closely tied to that of my favorite teacher, as I imagined her taking notes in his class, just as I would do in the fall.

Mrs. Belk was a gift to many of us students, but I will always remember her confident stride, her nifty tweed suits, the way she assumed we would do our best for her, and her never-failing excitement about plants, insects, and all forms of life. She believed in me, and that put a strong platform under my feet for all my future efforts.

Ann Turner

Ann Turner was born at the end of World War II and grew up in a liberal, book-crazed family in rural Massachusetts. With her father a printer and mother an artist, how could she not go into the creative arts? Ann wrote her first story at age eight and hasn't stopped since, writing primarily historical picture books, historical novels in the Dear America series, poetry, verse novellas, and more recently a memoir in verse, *Learning to Swim*. She has just completed a book about a bipolar girl set in the time of the Salem Witch Trials entitled *The Father of Lies.* She has two almost-grown children and a professor husband.

DON **KARDONG**

Olympic marathon runner

Discomfort as a Tool

People often remember teachers who made them feel special or empowered, educators who boosted self-esteem. But I remember one of my teachers for a much different reason. David Myers made me uncomfortable.

Mr. Myers was a Jesuit scholastic in training to become a priest. At Seattle Prep in the 1960s, he was both a classroom teacher and, during my senior year,

> **❝To this day, when I read something or watch a television show that references a concept in physics, I realize that my understanding and appreciation of that concept has its basis in an explanation Mr. Myers provided over four decades ago.❞**

the coach of the school's distance runners. That meant in the fall he was head cross-country coach, and in the spring assistant track coach.

I doubt if Mr. Myers's preferred subject was physics, and I have no idea how much of his background was in that area. But in the classroom he was exceptional, able to explain a complex concept simply and elegantly, and in a way that had staying power.

To this day, when I read something or watch a television show that references a concept in physics, I realize that my understanding and appreciation of that concept has its basis in an explanation Mr. Myers provided over four decades ago. How does a turbine generate electricity? Remember Myers's demonstration of a wire moving through an electrical field. What direction does the electricity flow? Remember the "rule of thumb." And so on.

None of that made me uncomfortable, but topics discussed during the rest of a typical physics class often did. Myers was acutely interested in things going on in the world, and a good chunk of each class period was spent discussing politics, social issues, and whatever else was making the news. Most of us came from comfortable middle-class backgrounds, and Myers had us face up to things many of us had never thought much about—racism, drug abuse, poverty, war. These were all hot topics at the time, and if you were in Myers's class it was impossible to ignore them.

Some of his approach was a reflection of Jesuit tradition, with its emphasis on a well-rounded education, social engagement, and the importance of core values. But Myers had a way of making those abstractions come alive. We used to joke that his physics classes were 5 minutes of physics and 45 minutes of politics. Whatever the truth of the time division, lessons from both parts of the class stuck. Why spend physics class time discussing current events? The message seemed to be that, whatever subject matter you were studying or life's work you eventually chose, it shouldn't be a way to alienate yourself from problems society was struggling with. And yes, that notion often made us uncomfortable.

Then too, there was his coaching, which he practiced with his own unique style. Myers wasn't the greatest student of distance running, but he worked us hard, and he used the sport like he did physics class, to educate and illuminate. One day he might urge us to dig deep, to "really want it," and the next, he might question the whole notion of competitive athletics. Many of the Native American runners he had worked with, he once told us, were more interested in the way running could nurture community than they were in beating each other. And wasn't that, he asked, more important? (Ouch, and just when I was feeling good about winning that race last Saturday . . .)

But maybe the most uncomfortable Mr. Myers ever made me was when he handed me a copy of a letter of recommendation I had requested for a college application. It was, as I eventually figured out, a parody of a letter of recommendation. I can't remember the exact words, but it would have been something along these lines: "Don is a good student who always comes to school with his homework done, his hair neatly combed, his teeth brushed, and his shoes shined." And so on, for an entire page, making me sound like the most insufferable Goody Two-Shoes on the planet.

I stood there reading his letter, appalled, with the deadline for sending in a completed application rapidly approaching. He let me sweat for a long, long time as I tried to fathom what he was up to. Then he handed over the real letter of recommendation.

The point? Well, he never actually explained it, so it may have just been a joke, a way to symbolically poke a graduating senior in the ribs. But I think there was a deeper message in his ploy. Perhaps, his trick suggested, I should ponder with a skeptical eye the whole process of applying for, being accepted by, and attending a university. If I was going to play the game, I should at least be aware that I was playing. That, too, made me uncomfortable.

For someone who had prodded me to question my future as a university student as well as my interest in competitive distance running, Myers had one final surprise in store. By the end of high school, I had lost much of my passion for running, and my performances suffered. I received no athletic scholarship offers, and I felt I was about done with running. Then one day Myers cornered me in the hall.

"You *are* planning to turn out in college, aren't you?" he asked.

In truth, I wasn't, or at least I hadn't made up my mind. But I was both startled and intimidated by his question. In a word, uncomfortable.

"Yes, I am," I heard myself saying. I just couldn't answer no.

And I did turn out. And found my passion for running again as a college freshman. And eventually made varsity. And continued to compete for years after graduating. So the teacher who once questioned the whole notion of competitive running set me on a course that eventually carried me all the way to the Olympic Games. If he hadn't decided to make me uncomfortable that one last time, none of that might have happened.

I haven't kept up with Mr. Myers over the years, but every once in a while I catch word of his doings. If the scuttlebutt is correct, he became a priest and a lawyer, and currently works on issues affecting Native Americans. And while I can't tell you for certain that all of that is true, I do know one thing for sure. Wherever he is and whatever he's up to, I know he's making a lot of people uncomfortable. Discomfort, as I'm sure he'd admit, can be quite an illuminating and effective tool.

Don Kardong grew up in Bellevue, Washington, and graduated from Stanford University in 1971. His running career has lasted over four decades, highlighted by a fourth-place finish in the 1976 Olympic marathon in Montreal. He is the founder and current race director of the Lilac Bloomsday Run in Spokane, a seven-and-a-half-mile footrace with nearly 50,000 participants each spring.

INDIRA **CESARINE**

Professional photographer

To Be Inspired, to Inspire

Education is something that in retrospect you realize shapes your life in ways unforeseen. As a student, one rarely is aware of the influence certain teachers may have upon you, or how later in life you are shaped by the support of certain teachers you may have had. I consider myself to be rather fortunate in my educational choices. At the age of 13, I made a rather unusual decision for a girl who grew up in Des Moines, Iowa. It was 1984, and with the influence of popular books like *The Official Preppy Handbook* raging throughout America, I decided that I wanted to go to an East Coast boarding school.

> **❝ To this day I can remember one teacher who I will always recognize as being truly supportive of my creativity . . . . After seeing the work I created at Parsons and in one of his classes, he created an independent study program for me, with access to a private darkroom on campus as well as a photographic studio space. ❞**

In Des Moines, the only students "sent away" to boarding school were those being punished for bad behavior, rather than being rewarded for academic excellence. I saw the move as an opportunity to find myself and to explore my own identity in an environment that would nurture my individuality rather than suppress it. With top PSAT scores in hand, and straight As throughout my classes, I applied to several boarding schools. My older sister accompanied me to my interviews, and the school that stood out the most was Choate Rosemary Hall, in Wallingford, Connecticut. The impressive school campus, strong support of the arts, and ethnic diversity of students inspired me.

Choate Rosemary Hall is a school famous for its legendary alumni, including John F. Kennedy, Paul Mellon, Michael Douglas, Glenn Close, and more recently, well-known alumni such as Ivanka Trump, as well as the sons and daughters of some top international leaders. I expected to be intimidated by the school and students but actually found the experience to be extremely rewarding. Going to class every day in buildings built by architects such as the celebrated I. M. Pei (renowned for the Pyramids of the Louvre) further inspired creative thought and made going to classes something to look forward to.

During the summer of 1986 I attended Parsons School for Design's summer program for high school students and studied photography in Manhattan; I discovered what would become for me a lifelong passion. I was immediately absorbed by the magic of photography. I found the process of developing film and printing photos allowed me to express myself in a way that I never could before. The spontaneous moments captured by still photography opened up a whole new world of expression.

To Be Inspired, to Inspire

To this day I can remember one teacher who I will always recognize as being truly supportive of my creativity, and that was John Faulkner, the head of the photography department at Choate Rosemary Hall. After seeing the work I created at Parsons and in one of his classes, he created an independent study program for me, with access to a private darkroom on campus as well as a photographic studio space at the Paul Mellon Art Center (built from the Endowment for the Arts made to Choate by the Mellon family). John Faulkner encouraged my independence, recognizing that I worked better on my own than in a class environment as I was so passionate about my work. In the program he created for me I worked in my own time and reported to him once a week to show him my photos. He encouraged advance darkroom and lighting techniques as well as medium-format work. Each term I presented an exhibit of my work with the subjects varying from portraiture and nudes to documentary-style images of New York nightlife.

By the time I graduated Choate, age 18, I had exhibited four one-woman shows at Choate's esteemed Paul Mellon Art Center, of my photography as well as mixed media of photography and painting. I graduated cum laude and was awarded the Choate Rosemary Hall award in Excellence in Photographic Art.

The summer after I graduated, in 1989, I presented my work to Elite Model Management in New York and started my career as a professional photographer. While completing a B.A. with a triple concentration in art history, French, and women's studies at Columbia College, Columbia University, I worked with many of the top New York and French modeling agencies. By 1993, I had my first major published series, ten pages in the London-based magazine *Don't Tell It*, as well as an exhibit of the work at the ultra-trendy Casa La Femme restaurant in New York. The past 16 years have flown by, marked by one assignment after another; I have worked internationally, in New York, Paris, London, Australia, Italy, and many exotic locations, for some of the world's most prestigious magazines and advertising clients. My upcoming work includes "The Goddess Manifesto," an international photographic installation and documentary focusing on my early work, as well as the launch of my own online magazine, *XXXX Magazine*, supporting multimedia art and collaborations between artists. Also, in 2009, I launched *Inspiration Organization*, a multimedia-based nonprofit group. Looking back at my experience working with John Faulkner has made me appreciate the independence he afforded me: he encouraged my independent study and allowed me access to facilities to hone my craft. I was lucky enough to be a student at Choate Rosemary Hall, and even more fortunate to have the encouragement of a teacher who recognized my need for expression and independence.

Indira Cesarine has been working as a fashion and beauty photographer for 20 years. A graduate of Columbia University, she started shooting for top modeling agencies in 1989 and has since been working with many international magazines, including *Vogue*, *In Style*, and *Marie Claire*. In addition to her photography, she is the fashion editor-at-large of *Lush* magazine and launched her own multimedia magazine, *XXXX Magazine*, in 2009. She is also well recognized from her appearances on the U.S. and UK versions of *Make Me a Supermodel*.

ANTHONY **BOZZA**

New York Times best-selling author

All Things Pass

Three words on a chalkboard. One man, standing before them, in his uniform: a simple tweed jacket, square tortoiseshell glasses, a button-down broadcloth shirt, silk bow tie, and well-worn brown leather shoes. It wasn't the first day of class and it

> **❝ The best lessons are never shouted. His have saved me more times than he'll ever know. ❞**

wasn't my first class with him, but that day he taught me more than any other teacher has ever taught me before or since. Those three words disseminated the wisdom he'd found in literature and in life more effectively than a library full of books could ever do. I'll forever be in awe and in debt to Mr. Frank Brogan for offering us the key to life as he saw it, so simply, so precisely, and so humbly. The best lessons are never shouted. His have saved me more times than he'll ever know.

Mr. Brogan was of average size, but his presence loomed large. He'd been a Marine in World War II and stormed the beach at Normandy. He did not tolerate any kind of misbehavior in his classroom. Those who made the mistake of causing a ruckus on his watch discovered that a keen mind and an observational eye are devastating weapons: Mr. Brogan made fools of class clowns and silenced chatterboxes with eloquent grace. He never brandished his power directly; he disarmed by dissection. He understood human nature, comprehending great works of literature as easily as he did the mind-set of his students. He wed the two with seamless aplomb. He strove to teach us that no matter how different they may be, all human stories share commonalities. At the end and in the beginning, after all, we are one and the same.

Mr. Brogan was feared more than he was adored. Those who understood what he was really teaching us revered him like no other. He lived as he taught: thoughtfully, seriously, and consistently. His wife worked in my school and on the chance occasion that she passed his classroom during the day, Mr. Brogan's face warmed with a smile befitting a love-struck teen. To see him giddy at the sight of her after so many years living and working beside each other was inspiring to me.

One day in my senior year, Mr. Brogan asked me to stay after class. There was no obvious reason: my grades were high, I participated regularly, and I never misbehaved (in his class, at least). But he saw what I'd been hiding: my parents' marriage was disintegrating. As an only child it was hard to bear. After the other students had left, he asked me quite directly how life was at home. He had a gaze like no one else I've ever met: his blue-gray eyes were as dense as polar ice, yet twinkled from within with the warmth of wisdom. For the next few minutes I enjoyed the freedom of true honesty. I hadn't told anyone about the fissure in my nuclear family and had no intention of ever doing so. Mr. Brogan, a teacher who'd taught me English for two years and observed me only within the confines of his class, had seen what I'd tried hard to hide, and cared enough to draw me out.

Mr. Brogan didn't offer easy solace, empathy, or coffee-table psychology; he shared the wisdom that had served him well through trials and tribulations more drastic than any I'd ever known. The best way to weather life's storms, he said, was to bury yourself in the right book.

I've followed my share of paths to freedom since then and that piece of advice has done me more good than the hours, dollars, and mental exertion I've spent elsewhere. The right book will open your eyes by being your mirror. With the right book in your hand, you will never be alone. When I finished college, the same year my parents finally divorced, I was entirely at sea, just another lost soul with a bachelor's degree. I sought structure and thought I'd find it in law school. It seemed a likely place to land. The summer before I made that decision, I sought out Mr. Brogan, who had retired from teaching.

He'd softened a bit since leaving the classroom, but his keen eyes had lost none of their luster. Sitting on his porch in his home, he fixed those eyes on me and once again became my teacher. He told me to read *1L* by Scott Turow. It's a memoir of the best-selling legal thriller author's first year as a student at Harvard Law. "It doesn't matter whether you like his fiction writing, Tony," Mr. Brogan said. "All you need to know about the experience of law school is in there. He captures it completely. Read it before you make any decisions. You'll know if law is right for you far before you reach the end."

Law wasn't for me, but it very well could have become my life. I sought a guaranteed refuge in a track to follow. For that I owe Mr. Brogan everything. He never told me what to be or do; he gave me the tools to learn who I am on my own. At that point in my life, I asked him a simple question and he gave me a simple answer. He reminded me of what he'd taught us all along. As important and critical as human folly might ever seem at the time, all things pass. We can build structures against what we see as chaos, but time will always win. In this life, we must be true to ourselves, because, in time, all things pass.

Anthony Bozza is a former *Rolling Stone* staff writer and the author of four *New York Times* best sellers. He grew up on Long Island and attended Friends Academy, one of several Quaker schools on the East Coast.

ELLIE **KRIEGER**

Host of *Healthy Appetite*, Food Network

He Made Me Feel Valued

Never underestimate small things. Sometimes they are what affect us most deeply and lastingly. My high school biology teacher didn't turn my life around or rescue me from horrible circumstances or become my closest friend. He simply took the time to listen one afternoon, and it stuck with me the rest of my life.

At my enormous, bustling New York City public high school, one-on-one conversations with teachers were usually rushed and to the point, sentences grabbed amid the din in the hall. I always felt more intimidated by my teachers than connected with them. Not so with Mr. Yohalem, who has a gentle kindness, playful approachability, and thoughtful wisdom about him. It was that demeanor and a tremendous respect for him that led me to turn to him for advice one afternoon.

> **He closed the door, sat down with me, and really listened! He carefully contemplated my options, explored my concerns, and offered me his wise suggestions. His generosity with his time was probably so ordinary for him he had no idea he was affecting me so meaningfully.**

Ellie Krieger

As a senior I faced a critical decision about which college to attend; I was confused about what would be best for me. When I approached Mr. Yohalem about my problem he did the most amazing thing. He closed the door, sat down with me, and really listened! He carefully contemplated my options, explored my concerns, and offered me his wise suggestions. His generosity with his time was probably so ordinary for him he had no idea he was affecting me so meaningfully. But he made me feel valued, like my future was something important and precious, and it stuck with me forever.

So teachers, know this: every day, you do small things that profoundly impact your students. Listening, believing, being a role model, taking the time to understand a child—seemingly ordinary acts that are truly extraordinary.

Ellie Krieger is a *New York Times* best-selling author. Ellie helps people of all ages achieve balance in food, health, and life, and have joy right at their fingertips. She is a registered dietitian and host of a hit show, *Healthy Appetite,* shown on the Food Network.

NICOLA **KRAUS**

New York Times best-selling coauthor, *The Nanny Diaries*

A World of Possibility

One would probably expect that, as a professional writer, I would want to use this opportunity to extol one of the many English teachers who encouraged my love of storytelling. And I am thankful for every one of them, but the teacher who changed my life taught me AP physics.

> **Under his guidance I became obsessed with this system that suddenly revealed the underpinnings of our world, from the vector of a gunshot to why an ambulance is at a higher pitch approaching you than receding (the Doppler effect).**

Now, like most creative types, I found that science was not a subject where my verbosity helped me, or endeared me to any teachers. I had essentially squeaked by, thinking of myself as an artist with no aptitude for math or science. But in 11th grade, forced to make the Solomonic decision between chemistry and physics, I chose physics. I'm still not sure why.

Mr. Eugene Gardino was our teacher and he brought to the class not only a crackling sense of humor, and a clear way of explaining things that made even subatomic particles comprehensible to a 16-year-old, but also a passion for the poetry of physics. Under his guidance I became obsessed with this system that suddenly revealed the underpinnings of our world, from the vector of a gunshot to why an ambulance is at a higher pitch approaching you than receding (the Doppler effect).

I have two favorite memories that inspire me to quote him often. In the first he was explaining to us that every step we take on the planet moves it backward, as it would if we were a clown walking on a rubber ball. But on the opposite side of the world someone is walking toward you and all our footsteps cancel each other out. Then someone asked, "But Mr. Gardino, what would happen if everyone lined up and took a step together?" He paused a brief moment, considering how to answer. "Well, then we could *really* get this sucker to roll." I still like to think of the earth that way, like a big rubber ball that could be totally under our control if only all of humanity could just agree on an action.

My second memory is from later in the year, when we had moved on to more advanced particle physics, and he was relating to us the facts of a famous experiment that I still read about in the *New York Times* Science section from time to time. A photon was fired through a surface with two slits into a metal wall that would record its position. The slits were opened and closed at random. In theory the proton should only have made it through, on average, half the time. *But the proton always made it through.* Somehow it course-corrected as if it had eyes. Mr. Gardino was staring out at 30 gobsmacked girls who couldn't have been more on the edge of our seats if he'd been telling a ghost story. "So, girls, the question is . . . " He paused dramatically. "How does the proton know?" It is a question that is still baffling physicists today.

A World of Possibility

The love of physics he engendered in me changed the way I thought about myself and how my brain worked. I never imagined in my twenties I would eagerly TiVo a Brian Greene special on *NOVA*. Or integrate concepts of string theory into my yoga practice. My English teachers nurtured my strengths, but Mr. Gardino exposed me to a world of possibility, both externally and internally, that I had never imagined.

Nicola Kraus is the coauthor of three *New York Times* best sellers: *The Nanny Diaries*, *Citizen Girl*, and *Dedication*. *The Nanny Diaries* was released as a motion picture in 2007, staring Scarlet Johansen. She and her partner, Emma McLaughlin, have also published a young adult novel, *The Real Real*; their newest novel, *Nanny Returns*, was published in December 2009.

Part Three

College

LESLIE **EPSTEIN**

Author, director of Creative Writing Program, Boston University

An Encouraging Figure

What I remember is a mélange of teachers, almost all of them associated with a certain fond feeling, but with a few bad apples as well. I know this much: I worked like the devil to get nothing but As for no other conscious reason than the wish not to disappoint these men and women.

> **❝I know his much: I worked like the devil to get nothing but As for no other conscious reason than the wish not to disappoint these men and women. ❞**

Perhaps the fact that my father died when I was young had something to do with it. Yet I was just as industrious before I turned 13. I encountered all of these folks in the Los Angeles school system until, a few years after my father's death in 1952, I went to the Webb School in Claremont.

Mrs. (*not* Ms.) Statek (whose name I have surely misspelled) was at Canyon Elementary—a place that was then made from World War II Quonset huts. It still is, thanks to Proposition Thirteen. Wild red hair, a dewlap, shaking jowls—and shaking a ruler, too. Was she the one who taped my mouth and made me sit in the corner? An excellent lesson, though I remained a wiseacre nonetheless.

Mrs. Edwards: short dark hair and a youthful beauty, who encouraged me to involve myself in the reelection campaign for the fine Mayor Fletcher Bowron. "Don't Be Behind the 'Times'"—then owned by the reactionary branch of the Chandler family—was our witty shared motto. Brentwood Elementary, perhaps.

Mr. Stegelmayer, Emerson Junior High: shiny cheeked, four eyed, with sprouts of hair sticking up in the back, he was an expert and interested history teacher. When I was bitching in my usual fashion about the old fogies who had written the Constitution, he admonished me: "Remember, they were wise enough to construct a means of changing their own document." That quieted me down. And I am sure he was the one (though in a novel about these years, I used poetic license to attribute the words to Gregory Peck) who told me, when I was still carrying on about the GOP, that the pendulum of history swung left and swung right; when it swung left, however, it always went a little bit further. Those same Republicans do not seem to have learned the laws of physics.

Mr. Edmondson, also at Emerson (or was it freshman year at University High?): tall, rather handsome, I think, and not old; his name and image have stuck in my mind because he was a kind and encouraging figure.

Ah, but Mr. Lindsay, probably at Emerson: yes, he inspired me to try to build a cyclotron (and to hang around the science labs at UCLA, where I was impressed by apples—not Newton's but the ones for sale in new automated machines), but he also pinched my ears and was known for doing so to other lads under his tutelage. Bit suspicious, eh what?

Worst of the lot was Ramsay Harris, who I think was part Malay, and who lived on to be a beloved figure aged 100 at the Webb School. He played the piano and made up lyrics for our school songs and taught God knows what. I never had him in the classroom, but one day I sat at his table for dinner; when the bursary student brought the mystery meat for the night, someone said, "What's *that*?"

"This week's profit," I replied (I told you the duct tape didn't work), and the next morning I was expelled. This same Harris, in one of his year-end poems, wrote, "Les's wit is as sharp as a persimmon/and rumor has it he don't like wimmen." This for distribution to the graduating class and their parents. I wish I were a tunesmith myself: "Old Ramsay pounds the keys to play oldies and blues/But he won't play Gershwin 'cause he don't like Jews." To think I went to the same college as Cole Porter.

But Webb had wonderful instructors: Fred Burr, who coached me in tennis and who had a fit when I only made the wait list at Yale. I never knew what all the fuss was about (I already had my room picked out at Columbia; for some reason I still think I remember it: 141 John Jay Hall) until I actually arrived in New Haven and discovered that not only weren't there many Jews, there weren't any wimmen. Mr. Sumner, quite aged, stained by nicotine, smelling of nicotine too, and spitting out tobacco juice as he taught us—and superbly—our lessons in French. *Restez dans la paix, mon vieux.* Jack Iversen, United States History, and a swell guy. And Sam Parkman, not that much older than his students, who strolled down my street in Brookline two years ago and whom I took, with his son, to a Red Sox game shortly after.

I won't dwell on Yale, except to say that in those days the best part of an education there was the endless lunches in the various colleges—in my case, Trumbull. Alas, the faculty isn't available for those repasts anymore, but in the late 1950s Charlie Blitzer and Chet Leib and Jim Hayden would sit with us from noon until we were thrown out at 3:30, day after day, shooting the breeze and teaching us (as all the fine people I have mentioned above taught us) how to put exactly one teaspoon of milk into our cups of coffee—in brief, how to become grown-up citizens in what all too soon would prove to be a difficult world.

P.S.: The wiseacre wasn't done. One day, lounging after one of those lunches on York Street, a few of us watched as the famous Richard Lee went into Phil the Barber's, then into Fenn Feinstein's, then Barrie's shoes. "What's the mayor doing?" asked one of my straight men. "Four o'clock on Friday," said I, glancing at my watch. "Time to collect." By ten the morning the next day I was thrown out of Yale, too. It was my tablemates, I believe, who arranged for me to stay in a house in nearby Hamden (thank you, Jim Hayden, though, sorry, I never learned how to play the recorder) instead of returning, rusticated, to California; and it was Charlie and Chet, in all likelihood, who mounted the campaign (stickers on walls and, finally, a story in the *New Haven Register*) that caused an abashed dean to call me with the words, "This has not been easy for any of us. Please return." When I wrote Richard Levin, the Yale president, a few years ago to beg him to reinstate the system that allowed faculty to live and eat in the colleges, he replied, "We are very proud of our college system." That non sequitur caused me to put him in the apple barrel too. Enough. It has been moving to think of these people. Thank you one, and, in truth, all.

Leslie Epstein had so many teachers he both loved and, occasionally, hated that he has become a loved and hated teacher himself—for the last 30 years at Boston University's Creative Writing Program. He's also written ten works of fiction and some plays.

LUTE **OLSON**

Former University of Arizona men's basketball coach

Cared About All of Us

I have been blessed to have many outstanding teachers through elementary and secondary schools and also in my college degree programs.

My story however is of a teacher who impacted my life when I was 34 years old and entering college coaching and counseling. Del Walker was the athletics director at Long Beach, California. He was a longtime teacher, coach, and administrator in the Long Beach School District for many years. He impacted more lives than any other person in the history of the district. He truly cared about everyone he met and did everything he could to help them to be the best they could be.

Del hired me in 1969 and was my mentor for many years until his passing in 2007. I will be indebted to him as long as I live.

Lute Olson

Lute Olson is the former men's basketball coach at the University of Arizona and the University of Iowa. Olson was known for player development, and many of his former players have gone on to impressive careers in the NBA after playing under him.

ROSANNE **CASH**

Grammy Award–winning singer and songwriter

Walter Taught Liberation

My favorite teacher was an English professor I had in college, at Vanderbilt University. His name was Walter Sullivan. I took his creative writing class. He was tough and didn't coddle the young writers under his tutelage, but he was also kind and articulate, and extraordinarily encouraging. I don't think I would have had the courage to write prose, had I not learned from Walter Sullivan. I am not afraid to take wild turns in a narrative, or allow myself to feel along in the dark for a surprise conclusion, because Walter taught liberation in the same breath that he taught structure. Walter probably has no idea how many writers have been influenced by him. I owe him an enormous debt, and I am tremendously grateful to have studied under him.

Rosanne Cash is an author and Grammy Award–winning singer and songwriter. Her 14 record albums, released over the last 30 years, have charted 11 No. 1 singles. She has earned numerous accolades for songwriting and performance.

PETER **COYOTE**

Actor, Emmy Award–winning narrator

His Dazzling Language

The most indelible impression a teacher ever left on me was my English professor at Grinnell College whose name was Sheldon Zitner. A small, round, owlish man with large horn-rimmed glasses, Zitner spoke slowly and carefully, with something of a high, querulous voice. He made absolutely no attempt to be charismatic, a regular guy, or a good buddy. His tweeds and sweater-vests were a bit musty and fuddy-duddy and there was nothing "hip" about him but the force of his mind and his dazzling use of English. Nevertheless, he changed my life. It was in his class one day that I realized, listening to him speak, that every word of English was and could be available for everyday discourse; that one did not need to dumb down one's communication, but in fact could expand it exponentially by treating the words one read in

> **❝It was in his class one day that I realized, listening to him speak, that every word of English was and could be available for everyday discourse; that one did not need to dumb down one's communication, but in fact could expand it exponentially by treating the words one read in books as a currency to be freely spent.❞**

books as a currency to be freely spent. I had a literal epiphany in his classroom one day, and felt the walls of my mind expand almost physically, and from that day forward have never discriminated between words that are spoken and words that are normally only written down.

His students were in awe of the sharpness and clarity of his mind and often traded "Zitnerisms" like baseball cards after class, collecting and swapping stories about the trenchant observations he would throw away in class like candy wrappers.

Two I remember particularly vividly. One day, when a student-athlete protested the professor's criticism of a certain writer, and defended the writer by asserting that he was "well-rounded," Zitner sighed and responded without hesitation, "Yes, he *is* well-rounded . . . and half an inch in diameter." On another occasion, during the study of Thucydides's *History of the Peloponnesian War*, he lowered his glasses, observed the class balefully, and said prophetically (though I did not fully understand it at the time), "Power is always, always, *always* . . . in the hands of the dumb, the blind, and the creepy." As my life has continued, the value and prophetic nature of Professor Zitner's comments and example have increased the value of his legacy to me.

Peter Coyote is an accomplished actor who has appeared in more than 90 films. He is an author, director, screenwriter, and an Emmy Award—winning narrator of films, theater, television, and audiobooks.

JERRY **SPINELLI**

Author and Newbery Medal winner, *Wringer*

On a Tangent

One of my favorite teachers at Gettysburg College was Dr. Francis Mason. The course was Survey of English Literature. Dr. Mason had a "problem" (self-professed): he couldn't stick to the subject of the day. He was always going out on a limb, off on, as he would say, "a tangent." Many times the class would be nearly over when he would glance at the clock in shock and discover that he had yet to cover the poem we had been assigned to study. If he said "I'm sorry" once, he said it a hundred times that year. I wish I had gone up to him after class one day and told him he didn't have to be sorry. His tangents—the fascinating ruminations between the lines of the assigned texts, the stuff we'd never find in a book—kept our interest in a way that no prospectus could. We left his classroom packed not merely with notebooks full of jottings but with hearts excited and inspired. He did something every student everywhere should be lucky enough to experience: he made us sorry the class was over.

Jerry Spinelli

Jerry Spinelli was born in Norristown, Pennsylvania, and graduated from Gettysburg College. His books are read in many languages and include *Maniac Magee,* winner of the Newbery Medal, and *Wringer,* a Newbery Honor Book. His wife is fellow writer Eileen Spinelli.

BILL **RODGERS**

Olympic marathon runner

My "Da," Charles Rodgers

My dad taught mechanical engineering for many years at a state college in Hartford, Connecticut. He was the best teacher I ever met. He taught me to value the small things in life, but most importantly my brother, Charlie, and I, and my sisters Martha and Linda learned that the world is an absolutely stunningly magical place—that exploration is everything.

My da, Charles Rodgers, was surprised, however, that none of us kids was very good at math!

I became a teacher of special-needs students years later, and then began my quest in the marathon all over the world.

Bill Rodgers is a runner and former American record holder in the marathon. He won both the Boston Marathon and the New York City Marathon in the late 1970s. In 1977, he won the Fukuoka Marathon, making him the only runner ever to hold the championship of all three major marathons at the same time. He made the 1976 U.S. Olympic team and raced the marathon at the Montreal Olympics in 1976.

MARK **CRILLEY**

Best-selling children's comics author, Akiko and Miki Falls series

Smiling from Ear to Ear

It was sometime in the fall of 1984, the beginning of my freshman year at Kalamazoo College. Vivian Dahlerup, a foreign exchange student from Denmark and one of the first friends I'd made on campus, had a tantalizing bit of news for me: "The artist-in-residence is doing a presentation in the Fine Arts Building this afternoon. You're such the artist, you really ought to be there." So it was that I met David Small.

I had no way of knowing how lucky I was. Though David had already begun to make a name for himself in children's books at that time, his first really big success, *Imogene's Antlers*, had only just been published and was not yet the beloved classic it was destined to become. I was lucky for

> **❝From our first one-on-one meeting I knew I'd found the mentor I'd been searching for throughout my teenage years. I brought all my very best drawings to David, the pictures that had won me praise from all quarters, and he riffled through them in about three minutes. ❞**

another reason, too: David's teaching years were nearing their end—his position was about to be eliminated—and I got to take what turned out to be his last two classes.

From our first one-on-one meeting I knew I'd found the mentor I'd been searching for throughout my teenage years. I brought all my very best drawings to David, the pictures that had won me praise from all quarters, and he riffled through them in about three minutes. "This one's nice," he'd say after having flipped past a dozen without comment. The final verdict: "You've got talent. But it's nothing that thousands of other people your age can't do. You really need to start working now." I call it the Great Creative Kick in the Pants. It was something I dearly needed, though it stung a bit at the time.

David wrote down the names of artists whose drawings I needed to study: da Vinci. Degas. Klimt. And off I went, doing study after study, trying to learn how to draw as the masters did.

By the end of my college years the teacher-student relationship had expanded into a full-blown friendship. I met David's wife, Sarah, joined them for the occasional restaurant meal, and eventually even spent the night at their home in the countryside. When a motor scooter accident landed me in the hospital, there was David to visit me, one of my student oil paintings tucked under his arm, reminding me of the work I'd need to get back to once my shattered thumb repaired itself.

After graduation, when I took off to teach English in Taiwan and Japan for a number of years, I kept in touch with David, mainly by mail. I'd send him photocopies of my drawings and get his handwritten responses, equal parts encouragement and criticism.

At one point I foolishly stopped writing, and for much of the 1990s we fell out of touch. When I heard on the radio that he'd won the Caldecott Medal, I finally put pen to paper and wrote to congratulate him. By then I had a few published books of my own and was able to mail him evidence of my efforts to follow in his footsteps. There were a few false starts, but eventually I got back into regular contact with him. A couple of years ago I was able to bring my wife and kids out to his place and introduce them to the man who remains the most important teacher I've ever had.

Just this past summer I visited David and Sarah. The three of us went out to dinner, and I told them the story of that day way back in 1984 when Vivian had brought me along to meet Kalamazoo College's artist-in-residence. David, as part of his presentation, had pulled out a poster from one of the college stage plays, a production of Henrik Ibsen's *Hedda Gabler*. It was clearly student work, but he saw much to admire in it: "You see?" he'd said. "You've got talented artists right here among you." How could I not be smiling from ear to ear? It was my poster.

"Goosebumps," Sarah said upon hearing me recount the tale, and presented evidence by way of an outstretched forearm. It's quite a story: the teacher singling out his future student for encouragement, even without knowing the young man was standing there in front of him. You'd almost think I'd made the whole thing up.

But I didn't.

Mark Crilley

Mark Crilley was raised in Detroit. After graduating from Kalamazoo College in 1988, he taught English in Taiwan and Japan for nearly five years. He began publishing his first comics series, Akiko, in 1995, which led to a popular series of chapter books from Random House. His work has been featured in *USA Today*, *Entertainment Weekly*, and on CNN *Headline News*. He lives in Novi, Michigan, with his wife, Miki, and children, Matthew and Mio.

ACKNOWLEDGMENT OF PERMISSIONS

The following sources have graciously granted permission to use their previously printed material.

Corgan, Billy, and The Smashing Pumpkins, "Porcelina of the Vast Oceans," *Mellon Collie and the Infinite Sadness*. p 1995 by Cinderella Music (BMI).

Glenn, John, with Nick Taylor, *John Glenn: A Memoir*. New York: Bantam Books, 1999.

Moyers, Bill, *Fooling with Words: A Celebration of Poets and Their Craft*. New York: William Morrow and Company, 1999.

ABOUT **THE EDITOR**

Holly Holbert was born and raised in Spokane, Washington. She is the youngest of five children. She graduated from Eastern Washington University with a degree in geography and elementary education. She met Bruce while attending the university. They were married in December 1985. She and Bruce live on six acres overlooking Long Lake on the Spokane River. They have three children: Natalie, 18; Luke, 17; and Jackson. 15. She is a stay-at-home mom.